The Battle for Somalia: Evaluating U.S. Military Interventions in the Fight Against Al-Shabaab

Copyright Page

TITLE: The Battle for Somalia: Evaluating U.S. Military Interventions in the Fight Against Al-Shabaab

1ST Edition

Copyright @ 2023

ISBN: 9798223650867

Table of Contents

The Battle for Somalia: Evaluating U.S. Military Interventions in the Fight Against Al-Shabaab

By Roberto Miguel Rodriguez

Chapter 1: U.S. Military Interventions in Somalia to Combat Extremist Group Al-Shabaab: An Evaluation

History and Background of U.S. Military Interventions in Somalia

The history of U.S. military interventions in Somalia is a complex and multifaceted one, characterized by a series of interventions aimed at combating the extremist group Al-Shabaab. Understanding the historical context and background of these interventions is crucial for military historians seeking to evaluate the effectiveness and success of U.S. efforts in Somalia.

The origins of Al-Shabaab can be traced back to the early 2000s, when it emerged as an offshoot of the Islamic Courts Union (ICU) in Somalia. The ICU, a coalition of Islamic courts that aimed to establish Sharia law in the country, gained control over large parts of southern Somalia. However, their rule was short-lived as they were overthrown by Ethiopian forces in 2006, with U.S. support.

Following the Ethiopian intervention, Al-Shabaab capitalized on the power vacuum and insurgency grew rapidly. The group quickly established a stronghold in southern Somalia and launched a series of attacks against government forces, African Union peacekeepers, and civilians. Their ideology is rooted in an extremist interpretation of Islam and they have sought to impose their version of Sharia law in areas under their control.

In response to the growing threat posed by Al-Shabaab, the United States initiated a series of military interventions in Somalia. These interventions have been primarily focused on providing support to the Somali government and its African Union partners in their efforts to combat Al-Shabaab. They have involved a combination of direct military action, such as targeted airstrikes and special operations raids, as well as training and advising Somali and African Union forces.

The U.S. counterterrorism strategies and tactics employed against Al-Shabaab have evolved over time. Initially, the emphasis was on direct military action, but this has gradually shifted towards a more holistic approach that includes efforts to build the capacity of the Somali security forces, promote governance and development, and counter the group's propaganda and recruitment efforts.

The impact of U.S. military interventions on the political landscape in Somalia has been significant. While they have helped weaken Al-Shabaab's operational capabilities, they have also faced criticism for inadvertently contributing to the destabilization of the country. Humanitarian consequences and civilian casualties have also been a concern, with reports of collateral damage and the displacement of civilians.

Assessing the long-term implications of U.S. military interventions in Somalia requires considering the role and involvement of regional actors. Countries such as Ethiopia, Kenya, and Uganda have contributed troops to the African Union Mission in Somalia (AMISOM) and have played a vital role in the fight against Al-Shabaab.

Moreover, the legal and ethical considerations surrounding U.S. military interventions are crucial. The use of targeted airstrikes and special operations raids raises questions about the legality and proportionality of these actions. Additionally, the impact on civilians and the potential for civilian casualties must be carefully considered.

Finally, it is essential to compare U.S. military interventions in Somalia with other counterterrorism campaigns in the region. Understanding the similarities and differences can provide valuable insights into the effectiveness of various approaches and strategies.

In conclusion, a comprehensive evaluation of U.S. military interventions in Somalia to combat Al-Shabaab requires a thorough understanding of the history and background of these interventions. By examining the origins of Al-Shabaab, the U.S. counterterrorism strategies employed, the impact on the political landscape, the humanitarian consequences, and the involvement of regional actors, military historians can gain valuable insights into the effectiveness and long-term implications of these interventions.

Early U.S. Involvement in Somalia

In this subchapter, we delve into the early U.S. involvement in Somalia, shedding light on its historical context and significance in the fight against the extremist group Al-Shabaab. As military historians, it is crucial to understand the roots of U.S. military interventions in Somalia to comprehensively evaluate their effectiveness and long-term implications.

The roots of U.S. involvement in Somalia can be traced back to the early 1990s when the country was engulfed in a devastating civil war. The collapse of the Siad Barre regime in 1991 led to a power vacuum, unleashing widespread violence and famine. The United States, along with other international actors, recognized the urgent need for humanitarian intervention. Operation Restore Hope, launched in 1992, aimed to provide aid and restore stability to the war-torn nation.

However, what was intended as a humanitarian mission soon evolved into a military one. The United States faced resistance from various Somali factions, including warlords who opposed foreign intervention. This resistance culminated in the infamous Battle of Mogadishu in 1993, also known as the Black Hawk Down incident. The battle showcased the challenges and complexities of intervening in Somalia and had a profound impact on U.S. military strategy in the region.

Following the Black Hawk Down incident, the United States shifted its approach in Somalia. Instead of deploying large ground forces, it focused on supporting regional actors and building indigenous security forces to combat Al-Shabaab. The U.S. military provided training, equipment, and intelligence support to African Union Mission in Somalia (AMISOM) troops, who were at the forefront of the fight against the extremist group.

The early U.S. involvement in Somalia laid the foundation for subsequent counterterrorism efforts against Al-Shabaab. It highlighted the importance of understanding the local dynamics and engaging with regional actors to achieve sustainable security outcomes. Furthermore, it underscored the need for a comprehensive strategy that integrates military, diplomatic, and humanitarian efforts.

As military historians, it is essential to critically analyze the early U.S. involvement in Somalia to assess its effectiveness and impact on the political landscape. This evaluation enables us to draw valuable lessons for future interventions and counterterrorism campaigns in the region. By examining the legal and ethical considerations surrounding U.S. military interventions and comparing them with similar campaigns, we can gain a comprehensive understanding of the complexities and challenges of combating extremist groups like Al-Shabaab.

U.S. Military Intervention in the 1990s and the Black Hawk Down Incident

The U.S. military intervention in Somalia during the 1990s, particularly the infamous Black Hawk Down incident, holds significant historical relevance in the evaluation of U.S. military interventions in the fight against Al-Shabaab. This subchapter aims to provide military historians with a comprehensive understanding of this critical period.

The United States' military involvement in Somalia began in 1992, with Operation Restore Hope. The primary objective was to provide humanitarian aid and restore stability to a country ravaged by civil war and famine. However, the mission soon escalated into a nation-building effort as the U.S. sought to establish a functioning government and combat the growing influence of warlords.

On October 3, 1993, the U.S. experienced a catastrophic event commonly known as the Black Hawk Down incident. During a mission to capture a prominent warlord, Somali militiamen shot down two U.S. Army Black Hawk helicopters, resulting in the deaths of 18 American soldiers and the capture of several others. The incident shocked the American public and had a profound impact on U.S. military strategy and tactics.

The Black Hawk Down incident highlighted the challenges faced by U.S. forces in Somalia, including limited intelligence, inadequate force protection, and an unfamiliar urban warfare environment. It prompted a reevaluation of U.S. military interventions and led to a shift in counterterrorism strategies.

Furthermore, the incident had profound implications for the political landscape in Somalia. The U.S. withdrawal following the incident left a power vacuum that allowed extremist groups like Al-Shabaab to flourish. This subchapter will explore the subsequent rise of Al-Shabaab and its origins, ideology, and operations in Somalia.

Additionally, it will examine the effectiveness and success of U.S. efforts in combating Al-Shabaab, considering the long-term implications of U.S. military interventions in Somalia. The involvement of regional actors, such as African Union forces, will be assessed to understand their role in supporting U.S. counterterrorism campaigns.

Moreover, this subchapter will delve into the legal and ethical considerations surrounding U.S. military interventions. It will critically analyze the humanitarian consequences and civilian casualties resulting from these interventions, providing a comprehensive evaluation of the impact on the Somali population.

Finally, a comparative analysis of U.S. military interventions in Somalia with other counterterrorism campaigns in the region will be presented. This will allow military historians to draw insightful parallels and identify lessons learned for future military interventions.

Overall, this subchapter aims to provide military historians with a comprehensive understanding of the U.S. military intervention in the 1990s and the Black Hawk Down incident, allowing for a critical evaluation of its impact on the fight against Al-Shabaab and the broader implications for U.S. military interventions in Somalia.

Renewed U.S. Involvement in Somalia in the 21st Century

In the 21st century, the United States has experienced renewed involvement in Somalia as part of its efforts to combat the extremist group Al-Shabaab. This subchapter aims to provide military historians with an evaluation of U.S. military interventions in Somalia and their impact on various aspects of the conflict.

To understand the current situation, it is crucial to examine the history and background of U.S. military interventions in Somalia. This includes an analysis of the initial intervention in the early 1990s and subsequent events that shaped the country's political landscape and security challenges.

Al-Shabaab, the primary target of U.S. interventions, originated as the youth wing of the Islamic Courts Union in the mid-2000s. Understanding its origins, ideology, and operations within Somalia is vital to comprehending the nature of the conflict.

The United States has employed various counterterrorism strategies and tactics to combat Al-Shabaab. Evaluating the effectiveness of these efforts is essential to assess the success of U.S. interventions and understand the challenges faced in countering this extremist group.

Moreover, the impact of U.S. military interventions on the political landscape in Somalia cannot be ignored. This subchapter will explore the consequences and civilian casualties resulting from these interventions, shedding light on the humanitarian aspects of the conflict.

To provide a comprehensive analysis, the involvement of regional actors in U.S. military interventions will be examined. Understanding their role and contribution can offer insights into the complexities of the conflict and the potential for regional cooperation.

Assessing the long-term implications of U.S. military interventions in Somalia is crucial to understanding the potential outcomes and consequences for both Somalia and the United States. This examination will consider the strategic, political, and security implications of continued involvement.

Moreover, legal and ethical considerations surrounding U.S. military interventions cannot be overlooked. This subchapter will delve into the legal framework within which these interventions operate, as well as the ethical dilemmas they present.

Lastly, a comparison of U.S. military interventions in Somalia with other counterterrorism campaigns in the region will be conducted.

This comparative analysis will provide valuable insights into the unique challenges and successes of U.S. efforts in Somalia.

In conclusion, this subchapter aims to provide military historians with a comprehensive evaluation of renewed U.S. involvement in Somalia in the 21st century. By examining various aspects of the conflict, from the history and background to the long-term implications, this analysis will contribute to a deeper understanding of U.S. military interventions in the fight against Al-Shabaab.

Al-Shabaab's Origins, Ideology, and Operations in Somalia

The subchapter "Al-Shabaab's Origins, Ideology, and Operations in Somalia" delves into the development and activities of the extremist group Al-Shabaab within the context of Somalia. This chapter aims to provide military historians with a comprehensive understanding of the group's roots, principles, and modus operandi.

Al-Shabaab, which translates to "The Youth" in Arabic, emerged as a radical offshoot of the Islamic Courts Union (ICU) in the early 2000s. Initially, the ICU sought to establish Sharia law in Somalia, but its extremist elements eventually formed Al-Shabaab, which adopted a more aggressive and militant approach. The group capitalized on the political vacuum in Somalia and exploited the country's fragile state institutions to expand its influence.

Ideologically, Al-Shabaab subscribes to a strict interpretation of Salafism, blending it with elements of Somali nationalism. The group aims to establish an Islamic state governed by its interpretation of Sharia law, rejecting any form of Western influence or democracy. Al-Shabaab's recruitment strategy targets marginalized and disenfranchised individuals, offering them a sense of purpose and belonging.

Al-Shabaab's operations in Somalia have had devastating consequences for the country and its people. The group has engaged in a wide range of activities, including guerrilla warfare, terrorist attacks, and the imposition of its harsh version of Islamic law. Al-Shabaab has targeted both domestic and international actors, such as the African Union Mission in Somalia (AMISOM) and Western interests, in an attempt to undermine stability and exert control.

The U.S. military interventions in Somalia to combat Al-Shabaab have been a crucial aspect of the battle against this extremist group. The chapter explores the various counterterrorism strategies and tactics employed by the United States, including drone strikes, training and equipping Somali security forces, and providing intelligence support to AMISOM. It also analyzes the effectiveness and success of these efforts, considering their impact on the political landscape in Somalia.

Additionally, this subchapter assesses the role and involvement of regional actors in U.S. military interventions, recognizing the importance of collaborative efforts in addressing the Al-Shabaab threat. It also discusses the humanitarian consequences and civilian casualties resulting from these interventions, emphasizing the need to balance security objectives with the protection of innocent lives.

Furthermore, the subchapter explores the long-term implications of U.S. military interventions in Somalia, examining the potential for sustainable stability and the challenges that lie ahead. Legal and ethical considerations surrounding U.S. military interventions are also examined, focusing on the adherence to international law and the moral implications of these actions.

Finally, the subchapter compares U.S. military interventions in Somalia with other counterterrorism campaigns in the region, providing military historians with a broader perspective on the strategic and operational aspects of these interventions.

Overall, this subchapter provides a comprehensive analysis of Al-Shabaab's origins, ideology, and operations in Somalia, offering military historians insights into the complexities and challenges faced by the United States and its allies in combating this extremist group.

Emergence of Al-Shabaab as a Militant Group

The emergence of Al-Shabaab as a militant group in Somalia has had profound implications for both the country itself and the broader region. Understanding the origins, ideology, and operations of Al-Shabaab is crucial in evaluating the effectiveness and success of U.S. military interventions in combating this extremist group.

Al-Shabaab, which means "The Youth" in Arabic, had its roots in the Islamic Courts Union (ICU), a group that aimed to establish an Islamic state in Somalia. Following the collapse of the central government in 1991, Somalia descended into chaos and lawlessness, providing fertile ground for the rise of extremist groups. The ICU gained control over large parts of southern Somalia in 2006, prompting U.S. concerns over the potential establishment of a safe haven for terrorists.

The ideological foundation of Al-Shabaab is rooted in a radical interpretation of Islam, influenced by Salafi-jihadist ideology. The group seeks to overthrow the fragile Somali government and implement its strict interpretation of Sharia law. Al-Shabaab has been responsible for numerous attacks targeting government officials, African Union peacekeepers, and civilians, both within Somalia and in neighboring countries such as Kenya and Uganda.

U.S. military interventions in Somalia to combat Al-Shabaab have primarily consisted of targeted drone strikes, special operations raids, and training and equipping Somali security forces. The counterterrorism strategies and tactics employed by the U.S. have focused on degrading Al-Shabaab's leadership, disrupting its operations, and building the capacity of Somali forces to counter the group.

However, the impact of U.S. military interventions on the political landscape in Somalia has been mixed. While the interventions have weakened Al-Shabaab to some extent, the group continues to pose a significant threat. Moreover, the interventions have also faced criticism for inadvertently causing civilian casualties and exacerbating humanitarian consequences in the country.

The involvement of regional actors, such as the African Union Mission in Somalia (AMISOM), has played a crucial role in supporting U.S. efforts. AMISOM, composed of troops from several African countries, has worked alongside Somali forces to combat Al-Shabaab and stabilize the country.

Assessing the long-term implications of U.S. military interventions in Somalia requires a comprehensive understanding of the legal and ethical considerations surrounding such interventions. Balancing the need to combat terrorism with the protection of civilian lives and adherence to international law remains a challenge.

Comparisons with other counterterrorism campaigns in the region, such as the U.S. interventions in Afghanistan and Iraq, can provide valuable insights into the effectiveness of U.S. efforts in Somalia. Lessons learned from these campaigns can inform future strategies and tactics in the fight against Al-Shabaab.

In conclusion, the emergence of Al-Shabaab as a militant group in Somalia has necessitated U.S. military interventions to combat its threat. Understanding the origins, ideology, and operations of Al-Shabaab is crucial in evaluating the effectiveness and success of these interventions. The role and involvement of regional actors, the impact on the political landscape, and the legal and ethical considerations surrounding these interventions all contribute to a comprehensive evaluation of U.S. efforts in Somalia.

Ideological Foundations of Al-Shabaab

The ideological foundations of Al-Shabaab have played a crucial role in shaping the extremist group's operations and its enduring presence in Somalia. Understanding these foundations is essential for military historians seeking to evaluate U.S. military interventions in the fight against Al-Shabaab.

Al-Shabaab, which means "The Youth" in Arabic, emerged in the early 2000s as an offshoot of the now-defunct Islamic Courts Union (ICU) in Somalia. Initially, the group presented itself as a nationalist movement opposing foreign intervention and advocating for the establishment of an Islamic state governed by strict Sharia law. However, over time, Al-Shabaab's ideology became more radicalized and aligned with global jihadist movements such as Al-Qaeda.

At its core, Al-Shabaab embraces a fundamentalist interpretation of Islam that seeks to establish a Caliphate in Somalia and beyond. The group believes in the necessity of armed struggle to achieve its objectives, viewing violence as a legitimate means to defend and propagate its version of Islam. Al-Shabaab justifies its attacks on both military and civilian targets as part of a broader jihad against perceived enemies, including Western powers, African Union forces, and the Somali government.

The group's ideology is characterized by a rigid interpretation of Islamic law, intolerance towards other religious or ideological beliefs, and a rejection of democratic governance. Al-Shabaab seeks to impose its own strict moral code on the population, forbidding activities such as music, sports, and even certain forms of dress. This has resulted in the group's brutal enforcement of its version of Islamic law, including public executions, amputations, and stonings.

Al-Shabaab's ideology has not only influenced its operations but has also attracted recruits and support from within Somalia and beyond. The group exploits grievances related to political marginalization, economic inequality, and clan rivalries to gain local support. Furthermore, its global jihadist ideology has enabled it to establish connections and receive support from other extremist groups, creating a transnational network that poses a significant threat to regional security.

In conclusion, the ideological foundations of Al-Shabaab have shaped the group's operations and its enduring presence in Somalia. As military historians evaluate U.S. military interventions in the fight against Al-Shabaab, understanding the group's origins, ideology, and operations is crucial. By comprehending the extremist group's ideological motivations, military strategists can develop more effective counterterrorism strategies to combat Al-Shabaab and mitigate its impact on the political landscape in Somalia. Additionally, analyzing the long-term implications of U.S. military interventions and comparing them with other counterterrorism campaigns in the region can provide valuable insights for future operations and policymaking.

Al-Shabaab's Strategies and Tactics in Somalia

As military historians delve into the complexities of U.S. military interventions in Somalia to combat the extremist group Al-Shabaab, it is crucial to thoroughly evaluate the strategies and tactics employed by this notorious organization. Al-Shabaab, which originated as a radical offshoot of the Union of Islamic Courts (UIC), has been a significant player in the political and security landscape of Somalia for over a decade.

One of the key strategies employed by Al-Shabaab is their ability to exploit the weak governance and security structures in Somalia. Capitalizing on the absence of a strong central government, they have established a parallel governance structure, imposing their own version of Islamic law and providing limited services to the local population. This strategy has allowed them to gain popular support, recruit new members, and create a safe haven for their operations.

In terms of tactics, Al-Shabaab has proven to be adaptive and resourceful. They have utilized a combination of guerrilla warfare, suicide bombings, and asymmetric attacks to target both military and civilian targets. Their use of improvised explosive devices (IEDs) has been particularly devastating, causing significant casualties and widespread fear among the population.

Furthermore, Al-Shabaab has successfully employed propaganda and social media as tools for recruitment and radicalization. They have exploited grievances and societal divisions to create a narrative of resistance against foreign intervention, portraying themselves as defenders of Islam and Somali nationalism. This has allowed them to attract fighters from Somalia and beyond, including individuals from the Somali diaspora in Western countries.

The U.S. military interventions in Somalia have sought to counter these strategies and tactics through a multi-faceted approach. This has involved targeted airstrikes against high-value targets, training and support for the Somali National Army and African Union Mission in Somalia (AMISOM) forces, and efforts to disrupt Al-Shabaab's financial networks. Additionally, the U.S. has utilized intelligence sharing and coordination with regional actors such as Kenya and Ethiopia to combat the group.

However, the effectiveness and success of these efforts have been mixed. While Al-Shabaab has suffered significant territorial losses and leadership setbacks, they have proven resilient and adaptable, regaining control over certain areas and launching high-profile attacks. Furthermore, the U.S. military interventions have had unintended consequences, including civilian casualties and humanitarian repercussions.

To fully understand the implications of U.S. military interventions in Somalia and their impact on the fight against Al-Shabaab, it is essential to assess the role and involvement of regional actors, as well as the legal and ethical considerations surrounding these interventions. Comparisons with other counterterrorism campaigns in the region can also provide valuable insights into the efficacy of different approaches.

In conclusion, an evaluation of Al-Shabaab's strategies and tactics in Somalia is crucial for military historians seeking to understand the complexities of U.S. military interventions in the fight against this extremist group. By analyzing the origins, ideology, and operations of Al-Shabaab, as well as the counterterrorism strategies employed by the U.S., historians can gain valuable insights into the effectiveness and long-term implications of these interventions. However, it is vital to consider the humanitarian consequences, civilian casualties, and broader political landscape in Somalia to provide a comprehensive evaluation.

U.S. Counterterrorism Strategies and Tactics Employed against Al-Shabaab

The ongoing battle against the extremist group Al-Shabaab in Somalia has necessitated the implementation of various counterterrorism strategies and tactics by the United States. This subchapter will delve into the intricacies of these efforts, shedding light on their effectiveness, impact, and long-term implications.

The United States has adopted a multifaceted approach to combat Al-Shabaab, combining military operations, intelligence gathering, and partnerships with regional actors. One of the key strategies employed is targeted airstrikes, aimed at eliminating high-value Al-Shabaab leaders and disrupting their operations. These airstrikes, carried out by both manned and unmanned aircraft, have played a crucial role in weakening the group's command structure and impeding its ability to plan and execute attacks.

In addition to airstrikes, the U.S. has deployed Special Operations Forces (SOF) to train and assist Somali security forces in their fight against Al-Shabaab. This strategy seeks to enhance the capabilities of local forces, enabling them to effectively counter the group's insurgency. The U.S. has also provided logistical support, intelligence sharing, and equipment to bolster the Somali government's capacity to combat Al-Shabaab.

Furthermore, the U.S. has invested in intelligence gathering and analysis to better understand Al-Shabaab's operations and identify potential threats. This includes surveillance and reconnaissance missions, as well as partnerships with regional intelligence agencies to exchange information and coordinate efforts. Such intelligence-driven operations have proven instrumental in disrupting Al-Shabaab's networks and preventing attacks.

However, it is important to consider the impact of these counterterrorism strategies on the political landscape in Somalia. The presence of U.S. forces and their involvement in military interventions have generated both support and criticism within the country. While some argue that U.S. assistance has contributed to the weakening of Al-Shabaab and stabilization of the government, others raise concerns about violations of sovereignty and the potential for civilian casualties.

The humanitarian consequences and civilian casualties resulting from U.S. military interventions in Somalia cannot be ignored. While efforts are made to minimize civilian harm, the complex nature of counterterrorism operations in urban areas poses significant challenges. It is essential to evaluate the humanitarian impact of these interventions and take steps to mitigate civilian casualties and address the needs of affected populations.

To assess the effectiveness and success of U.S. efforts in combating Al-Shabaab, it is crucial to analyze not only the military gains but also the broader socio-political context. This evaluation should consider factors such as the root causes of extremism, governance and state-building efforts, and the role of regional actors in supporting or hindering U.S. objectives.

By critically examining U.S. counterterrorism strategies and tactics employed against Al-Shabaab, this subchapter aims to provide military historians with a comprehensive understanding of the complexities surrounding U.S. military interventions in Somalia. It underscores the need for a holistic evaluation that considers the historical, political, ethical, and long-term implications of these interventions, in comparison with other counterterrorism campaigns in the region.

Direct Military Action against Al-Shabaab

Direct military action has been a key component of the United States' efforts to combat the extremist group Al-Shabaab in Somalia. This subchapter will delve into the various aspects of these military interventions, evaluating their effectiveness and success, as well as their impact on the political landscape in Somalia.

The decision to employ direct military action against Al-Shabaab was driven by the group's origins, ideology, and operations within Somalia. Al-Shabaab emerged in the early 2000s as an offshoot of the Islamic

Courts Union, with the goal of establishing an Islamic state governed by a strict interpretation of Sharia law. Over the years, Al-Shabaab has carried out numerous attacks targeting both Somali citizens and international actors, including the infamous Westgate Mall attack in Nairobi, Kenya.

U.S. counterterrorism strategies and tactics employed against Al-Shabaab have included airstrikes, drone strikes, and special operations raids targeting high-value individuals within the group's leadership. These efforts have sought to disrupt Al-Shabaab's operational capabilities and degrade its ability to carry out attacks. However, the effectiveness of these tactics in eliminating or significantly weakening the group has been a subject of debate among military historians.

While direct military action has had some success in killing key leaders and disrupting the group's infrastructure, it has also had unintended consequences. The humanitarian consequences of these interventions cannot be overlooked, as civilian casualties have occurred during airstrikes and other military operations. Such incidents have raised ethical and legal concerns surrounding the use of force in counterterrorism campaigns.

Furthermore, the involvement of regional actors, such as the African Union Mission in Somalia (AMISOM), has been crucial in supporting and supplementing U.S. military interventions. AMISOM, composed of troops from various African countries, has worked alongside U.S. forces to combat Al-Shabaab and stabilize the country. Their collaboration and cooperation have been instrumental in the overall success of the interventions.

As military historians, it is essential to assess the long-term implications of U.S. military interventions in Somalia. While these interventions have had short-term successes in weakening Al-Shabaab, they have not eradicated the group entirely. Additionally, the interventions have influenced the political landscape in Somalia, shaping alliances and power dynamics within the country.

To gain a comprehensive understanding of U.S. military interventions in Somalia, it is important to compare them with other counterterrorism campaigns in the region. By examining similarities and differences in strategies, tactics, and outcomes, we can draw valuable lessons and insights that can inform future military interventions against extremist groups.

In conclusion, direct military action against Al-Shabaab has been a central component of U.S. efforts to combat the group in Somalia. While these interventions have achieved some successes, they have also raised humanitarian concerns and had long-term implications on the political landscape of the country. By evaluating and analyzing these interventions, military historians can contribute to a deeper understanding of the challenges and complexities surrounding counterterrorism campaigns in the region.

Support for Somali National Security Forces

One crucial aspect of U.S. military interventions in the fight against Al-Shabaab in Somalia has been the support provided to the Somali National Security Forces (SNSF). The SNSF comprises the Somali National Army, the Somali Police Force, and the National Intelligence and Security Agency. The U.S. has played a significant role in training, equipping, and advising the SNSF to enhance their capacity to combat Al-Shabaab and establish stability in Somalia.

The support for the SNSF has been multifaceted. Firstly, the U.S. has invested heavily in military training programs for Somali soldiers and police officers. Through programs like the African Contingency Operations Training and Assistance (ACOTA), the U.S. has trained thousands of Somali troops in basic infantry skills, counterterrorism tactics, and leadership development. These training programs aim to enhance the effectiveness and professionalism of the SNSF, enabling them to better confront the threat posed by Al-Shabaab.

In addition to training, the U.S. has provided significant military aid to the SNSF. This includes the provision of weapons, ammunition, vehicles, and other equipment necessary for counterinsurgency operations. The U.S. has also assisted in the establishment of command and control structures within the SNSF, facilitating coordination and communication between different units. By equipping the SNSF with modern and effective tools, the U.S. aims to enhance their operational capabilities and increase their chances of success against Al-Shabaab.

Furthermore, the U.S. has provided advisory support to the SNSF, with American military advisors embedded within Somali units. These advisors offer guidance, expertise, and strategic advice to the SNSF, assisting them in planning and executing operations against Al-Shabaab. The advisory support is crucial in helping the SNSF build their own capabilities, develop effective strategies, and improve their overall performance.

The support for the SNSF is not without challenges. The Somali security forces have faced issues such as corruption, lack of discipline, and factionalism. Addressing these challenges is necessary to ensure the long-term success of U.S. military interventions. Efforts to improve the SNSF's accountability and professionalism are essential to build a capable and sustainable security apparatus in Somalia.

Overall, the support provided to the SNSF by the U.S. has been instrumental in the fight against Al-Shabaab. By training, equipping, and advising the Somali security forces, the U.S. aims to enhance their capacity to counter the extremist group and establish stability in

Somalia. However, sustained efforts are required to address the challenges faced by the SNSF and ensure their long-term effectiveness.

Intelligence and Surveillance Operations

In the battle against Al-Shabaab, intelligence and surveillance operations have played a crucial role in the U.S. military interventions in Somalia. This subchapter will delve into the significance of these operations, highlighting their impact on the overall effectiveness and success of U.S. efforts in combating Al-Shabaab.

Intelligence gathering has been a cornerstone of counterterrorism strategies employed by the U.S. military in Somalia. Through various means, including human intelligence, signals intelligence, and imagery intelligence, the U.S. military has sought to understand and disrupt Al-Shabaab's operations. By closely monitoring the extremist group's communications, activities, and networks, intelligence agencies have been able to provide critical information to inform military operations and target Al-Shabaab leaders.

Surveillance operations have also been instrumental in tracking and monitoring the movements of Al-Shabaab fighters. Through the use of advanced technology, such as drones and satellites, the U.S. military has been able to conduct real-time surveillance, gathering valuable information on the group's activities and identifying potential targets. This has allowed for precision strikes and the disruption of Al-Shabaab's operations, reducing its ability to carry out attacks.

However, intelligence and surveillance operations have not been without challenges. Al-Shabaab has proven to be a highly adaptable adversary, employing tactics such as encryption and decentralized command structures to evade detection. Moreover, the vast and rugged terrain of Somalia has posed logistical challenges for surveillance operations, requiring the U.S. military to constantly adapt and innovate its capabilities.

The effectiveness of intelligence and surveillance operations can also be evaluated in terms of their impact on the political landscape in Somalia. By targeting Al-Shabaab leaders and disrupting their activities, the U.S. military has sought to weaken the group's influence and create space for the Somali government to assert control. However, critics argue that the reliance on military force, including drone strikes, may have inadvertently fueled anti-American sentiment and radicalization among the local population.

Furthermore, the ethical considerations surrounding intelligence and surveillance operations cannot be overlooked. The U.S. military has faced criticism for potential civilian casualties resulting from these operations. The delicate balance between disrupting Al-Shabaab and minimizing harm to innocent civilians remains a challenge, one that requires constant reassessment and adherence to international norms and laws.

In comparing U.S. military interventions in Somalia with other counterterrorism campaigns in the region, intelligence and surveillance operations have been a common thread. However, the unique dynamics of Somalia, including its complex clan-based politics and porous borders, present distinct challenges that require tailored approaches.

In conclusion, intelligence and surveillance operations have played a critical role in the U.S. military interventions in Somalia. Their effectiveness in disrupting Al-Shabaab's operations and minimizing harm to civilians must be carefully evaluated. Furthermore, the long-term implications of these operations, both in terms of their impact on the political landscape in Somalia and the broader counterterrorism efforts in the region, warrant ongoing analysis and assessment.

Impact of U.S. Military Interventions on the Political Landscape in Somalia

The Impact of U.S. Military Interventions on the Political Landscape in Somalia

The political landscape in Somalia has undergone significant transformations as a result of U.S. military interventions aimed at combating the extremist group Al-Shabaab. These interventions have played a crucial role in shaping the country's political dynamics, both positively and negatively.

One of the key impacts of U.S. military interventions has been the weakening of Al-Shabaab's influence over large parts of Somalia. Through targeted airstrikes, drone operations, and support for the Somali National Army, the U.S. has significantly degraded the capabilities of Al-Shabaab, liberating territories previously under their control. This has allowed the Somali government to extend its authority and establish a semblance of stability in these areas.

However, the interventions have also had unintended consequences. The use of force by the U.S. military has resulted in civilian casualties and humanitarian consequences. While the U.S. has made efforts to minimize civilian harm, the complex nature of the conflict and Al-Shabaab's tactics have made it challenging to prevent collateral damage. These civilian casualties have led to resentment and anger among the Somali population, potentially fueling support for Al-Shabaab.

Moreover, the involvement of the U.S. in Somalia has raised questions about the legal and ethical considerations surrounding military interventions. Critics argue that the U.S. interventions have violated Somalia's sovereignty and international law. The use of targeted killings and drone strikes without clear legal frameworks has raised concerns about accountability and transparency.

The long-term implications of the U.S. military interventions in Somalia also warrant examination. While these interventions have weakened Al-Shabaab, the underlying factors that contributed to the rise of the extremist group, such as political instability, poverty, and clan divisions, remain largely unaddressed. The U.S. must work in conjunction with regional actors and the Somali government to develop comprehensive strategies that address these root causes and prevent the resurgence of extremist groups in the future.

In conclusion, U.S. military interventions in Somalia have had a significant impact on the country's political landscape. While they have successfully weakened Al-Shabaab, they have also resulted in civilian casualties, raised legal and ethical concerns, and failed to address the underlying causes of extremism. It is crucial for military historians and policymakers to evaluate the effectiveness and long-term implications of these interventions to inform future counterterrorism campaigns in the region.

Effects on the Somali Government and Institutions

The U.S. military interventions in Somalia to combat the extremist group Al-Shabaab have had profound effects on the Somali government and institutions. These effects can be analyzed from various perspectives, including political, institutional, and socio-economic.

One of the major impacts of U.S. military interventions has been on the political landscape in Somalia. Prior to these interventions, the country was plagued by a lack of stability and weak governance. The presence of Al-Shabaab hindered the government's efforts to establish control over the entire territory. However, with the support of the U.S. military,

Somali government forces have been able to reclaim significant areas from the control of Al-Shabaab. This has led to the establishment of a more stable political environment in parts of the country.

Institutionally, the Somali government has received assistance from the U.S. military in terms of capacity building and training. This has helped strengthen the Somali security forces and improve their effectiveness in combating Al-Shabaab. The interventions have also facilitated the establishment of a more efficient and organized military structure within the Somali government, enabling it to better respond to security threats.

On the socio-economic front, the U.S. military interventions have had mixed effects. On one hand, the interventions have disrupted Al-Shabaab's operations, which has allowed for the delivery of humanitarian aid to areas previously controlled by the extremist group. This has alleviated some of the suffering of the Somali population and contributed to improved living conditions. On the other hand, the interventions have also resulted in civilian casualties and displacement, causing further hardships for the Somali people.

Furthermore, the interventions have led to the involvement of regional actors in Somalia. Countries like Kenya and Ethiopia have played significant roles in supporting the Somali government's efforts to combat Al-Shabaab. This regional involvement has both positive and negative implications, as it can contribute to stability and security, but it can also complicate the political dynamics and increase the risk of regional conflicts.

In conclusion, the U.S. military interventions in Somalia have had wide-ranging effects on the Somali government and institutions. While they have contributed to improvements in the political and security landscape, there have also been negative consequences, particularly in terms of civilian casualties and displacement. It is important for military historians to evaluate these effects and consider the long-term implications of U.S. interventions in Somalia, especially in comparison to other counterterrorism campaigns in the region. Additionally, the legal and ethical considerations surrounding these interventions should be analyzed to ensure that future interventions are conducted in a manner that minimizes harm to civilians and respects international norms.

Influence on Regional and Local Power Dynamics

The influence of U.S. military interventions in Somalia on regional and local power dynamics has been a significant aspect of the battle against the extremist group Al-Shabaab. Understanding the impact of these interventions is crucial in evaluating the effectiveness and success of U.S. efforts in combating terrorism in the region.

One of the key aspects to consider is the role and involvement of regional actors in U.S. military interventions. Somalia has long been a complex web of political and tribal dynamics, and the presence of external forces has the potential to disrupt these delicate balances. Regional actors, such as neighboring countries and international organizations, play a critical role in shaping the outcome of U.S. military interventions. Their support, or lack thereof, can significantly impact the effectiveness of counterterrorism strategies and tactics employed against Al-Shabaab.

Moreover, U.S. military interventions have had a direct impact on the political landscape in Somalia. These interventions have often been accompanied by efforts to build and strengthen the Somali government and security forces. While this has been a necessary step towards stability, it has also created power struggles and tensions within the country. The influence of external forces on the local power dynamics can either enhance or undermine the legitimacy and authority of the Somali government, depending on the approach taken.

Additionally, the humanitarian consequences and civilian casualties of U.S. military interventions cannot be overlooked. While the primary goal is to combat Al-Shabaab and ensure the safety and security of the Somali people, the use of military force inevitably leads to collateral damage. It is essential to critically analyze the humanitarian impact of these interventions and assess whether the benefits outweigh the costs.

Examining the long-term implications of U.S. military interventions in Somalia is also crucial. While short-term gains may be achieved, it is essential to assess the sustainability of these interventions and the potential for lasting positive change. The influence on regional and local power dynamics must be considered in this assessment, as it can shape the future trajectory of the country and its ability to combat extremism effectively.

Finally, legal and ethical considerations surrounding U.S. military interventions cannot be ignored. The adherence to international law and respect for human rights must be central to any counterterrorism campaign. Evaluating the extent to which the U.S. interventions have upheld these principles is vital in understanding their overall impact.

By comparing U.S. military interventions in Somalia with other counterterrorism campaigns in the region, military historians can gain valuable insights into the effectiveness and success of these interventions. This comparative analysis allows for a broader perspective and highlights the unique challenges and opportunities presented by the Somali context.

Overall, evaluating the influence of U.S. military interventions on regional and local power dynamics provides a comprehensive understanding of the complex dynamics at play in the battle against Al-Shabaab. It allows for a nuanced assessment of the effectiveness and long-term implications of these interventions, ensuring that future strategies can be informed by lessons learned from the past.

Challenges in Establishing a Stable Political Climate

One of the most significant challenges in establishing a stable political climate in Somalia lies in the complex and intricate nature of the country's political landscape. The Battle for Somalia: Evaluating U.S. Military Interventions in the Fight Against Al-Shabaab delves into the numerous obstacles faced by both the United States and Somalia in their efforts to create a stable political environment.

One of the primary challenges stems from the fragmented nature of Somalia's political structure. The country has been ravaged by civil war and internal conflicts for decades, resulting in the emergence of various clans, warlords, and factions vying for power. These divisions have hindered the establishment of a centralized government, making it difficult to create a cohesive political system that can effectively address the needs and aspirations of the Somali people.

Another challenge lies in the presence and influence of Al-Shabaab, an extremist group that has posed a significant threat to Somalia's stability. The origins, ideology, and operations of Al-Shabaab are explored in detail, shedding light on the complexities involved in combating this group. The book evaluates the strategies and tactics employed by the United States in countering Al-Shabaab, assessing their effectiveness and success.

The impact of U.S. military interventions on the political landscape in Somalia is also examined. While these interventions have aimed to weaken Al-Shabaab and bolster the Somali government, they have also faced significant criticism for their humanitarian consequences and civilian casualties. The book analyzes these consequences and explores the ethical and legal considerations surrounding U.S. military interventions.

Furthermore, the role and involvement of regional actors in U.S. military interventions are evaluated, providing a comprehensive understanding of the broader geopolitical dynamics at play in Somalia. The long-term implications of these interventions are assessed, considering their effects on regional stability and security.

By comparing U.S. military interventions in Somalia with other counterterrorism campaigns in the region, the book offers valuable insights into the unique challenges faced in Somalia and the lessons that can be learned from past experiences.

Overall, "The Battle for Somalia" provides military historians with a comprehensive evaluation of U.S. military interventions in Somalia to combat Al-Shabaab. By examining the challenges in establishing a stable political climate, the book offers a nuanced understanding of the complexities involved and the implications for both Somalia and the United States.

Humanitarian Consequences and Civilian Casualties of U.S. Military Interventions

In the ongoing battle against Al-Shabaab in Somalia, the United States has played a significant role in supporting the Somali government and its military forces. However, it is crucial to evaluate the humanitarian consequences and civilian casualties that have resulted from these U.S. military interventions. This subchapter aims to shed light on this critical aspect of the conflict and provide a comprehensive analysis for military historians and those interested in U.S. military interventions in Somalia.

When examining the impact of U.S. military interventions on civilian populations, it is essential to acknowledge the complexity of the conflict in Somalia. Al-Shabaab's tactics, which often involve blending in with civilian communities and using them as shields, have made it challenging to minimize civilian casualties. Despite the efforts taken by the U.S. military to employ precision strikes and minimize collateral damage, instances of civilian casualties have occurred.

The consequences of these casualties are far-reaching. Not only do they result in the loss of innocent lives, but they also have the potential to undermine the legitimacy of the U.S. military interventions and fuel anti-American sentiments among the Somali population. Additionally, civilian casualties can create a breeding ground for further radicalization and recruitment for extremist groups like Al-Shabaab.

To address these concerns, it is necessary to explore the strategies employed by the U.S. military in mitigating civilian casualties. This includes examining the use of advanced intelligence capabilities, targeted operations, and coordination with local forces. By analyzing the effectiveness of these strategies, military historians can gain valuable insights into the challenges and limitations faced by the U.S. military in its fight against Al-Shabaab.

Furthermore, this subchapter will delve into the legal and ethical considerations surrounding U.S. military interventions in Somalia. It will explore the adherence to international humanitarian law and the principles of proportionality and distinction. By critically evaluating the U.S. military's compliance with these standards, military historians can assess the ethical implications of their actions.

Ultimately, the analysis of the humanitarian consequences and civilian casualties resulting from U.S. military interventions in Somalia is crucial for understanding the broader impact of these operations. By examining both the short-term and long-term implications, military historians can contribute to a more comprehensive evaluation of the effectiveness and success of U.S. efforts in combating Al-Shabaab. Additionally, a comparison with other counterterrorism campaigns in the region will provide valuable insights into the unique challenges faced in Somalia and the lessons that can be learned for future military interventions.

Collateral Damage and Civilian Casualties

In the battle against the extremist group Al-Shabaab in Somalia, the United States has employed various military interventions. However, with these interventions come the unfortunate consequences of collateral damage and civilian casualties. This subchapter aims to evaluate the impact of U.S. military interventions on the humanitarian landscape and the lives of civilians in Somalia.

When examining the collateral damage caused by U.S. military interventions, it is crucial to understand the complex nature of the conflict. Al-Shabaab's operations in Somalia often blend with civilian populations, using them as shields or exploiting their vulnerabilities. As a result, U.S. counterterrorism strategies and tactics, such as drone strikes or targeted operations, can inadvertently lead to civilian casualties.

The humanitarian consequences of U.S. military interventions are far-reaching. Not only are innocent lives lost, but the destruction of infrastructure, homes, and livelihoods exacerbates the already dire humanitarian situation in Somalia. Moreover, the displacement of civilians due to the violence further strains the limited resources of humanitarian organizations and increases the risk of famine and disease outbreaks.

Assessing the effectiveness and success of U.S. efforts in combating Al-Shabaab requires a nuanced understanding of the long-term implications. While military interventions may degrade Al-Shabaab's capabilities and disrupt their operations, they often fail to address the root causes of extremism. Without comprehensive strategies that address governance, economic development, and political stability, military interventions alone may not achieve lasting success.

The involvement of regional actors in U.S. military interventions is also noteworthy. Countries like Kenya, Ethiopia, and Uganda have played significant roles, contributing troops to the African Union Mission in Somalia (AMISOM). Understanding their motivations, strategies, and challenges is crucial for comprehending the wider regional dynamics and their impact on the effectiveness of U.S. interventions.

Legal and ethical considerations surrounding U.S. military interventions are essential to evaluate the legitimacy of such actions. Questions regarding the authorization of force, adherence to international humanitarian law, and the proportionality of military actions are crucial in assessing the ethical implications of collateral damage and civilian casualties.

Finally, comparing U.S. military interventions in Somalia with other counterterrorism campaigns in the region provides valuable insights into the successes and failures of various approaches. By examining interventions in countries like Afghanistan or Iraq, military historians can draw parallels and learn from past experiences to inform future strategies in combating extremist groups.

In conclusion, the collateral damage and civilian casualties resulting from U.S. military interventions in Somalia have had significant humanitarian consequences. Understanding and evaluating the impact on the political landscape, the effectiveness of counterterrorism strategies, and the involvement of regional actors are crucial in assessing the long-term implications of these interventions. Furthermore, analyzing the legal and ethical considerations and comparing interventions in the region can provide valuable lessons for future military operations.

Displacement and Humanitarian Crisis

The subchapter titled "Displacement and Humanitarian Crisis" delves into the significant impact of U.S. military interventions in Somalia on displacement and the ensuing humanitarian crisis. This section aims to provide military historians with a comprehensive understanding of the consequences of these interventions, shedding light on the complexities of the situation and the challenges faced by both the Somali population and humanitarian actors.

Since the early 1990s, Somalia has been plagued by conflict, political instability, and the rise of extremist group Al-Shabaab. U.S. military interventions were initiated with the primary objective of combating this terrorist organization and stabilizing the region. However, the unintended consequences of these interventions have resulted in a severe displacement crisis and exacerbated the already fragile humanitarian situation.

The displacement crisis in Somalia has been characterized by the forced displacement of millions of people, both internally and across borders. The conflict, combined with Al-Shabaab's brutal tactics, has led to widespread displacement, with civilians fleeing their homes in search of safety. Displacement camps have emerged, housing thousands of vulnerable individuals who lack access to basic necessities, such as food, water, and healthcare.

Moreover, U.S. military interventions have had direct or indirect impacts on civilian casualties. The use of airstrikes and military operations, while intending to target Al-Shabaab, has often resulted in unintended civilian casualties. This has further exacerbated the humanitarian crisis and strained the relationship between the local population and foreign forces.

Humanitarian actors, including international organizations and non-governmental organizations, have been mobilized to address the growing needs of those affected by displacement and the humanitarian crisis. However, the volatile security situation, limited access to affected areas, and the politicization of aid delivery have hindered their efforts.

To evaluate the effectiveness and success of U.S. efforts in combating Al-Shabaab, it is crucial to assess the impact on the humanitarian landscape. By analyzing the displacement crisis and the resulting humanitarian consequences, military historians can gain insights into the wider implications of U.S. military interventions in Somalia.

Furthermore, this subchapter will also explore the legal and ethical considerations surrounding U.S. military interventions, examining whether these interventions adhere to international humanitarian law and human rights standards. By comparing U.S. interventions in Somalia with other counterterrorism campaigns in the region, military historians can gain a broader perspective on the challenges and potential lessons learned.

In conclusion, the subchapter on "Displacement and Humanitarian Crisis" provides military historians with a comprehensive analysis of the consequences of U.S. military interventions in Somalia. By examining the displacement crisis, civilian casualties, and the humanitarian response, this section sheds light on the complexities and challenges faced in the fight against Al-Shabaab. Understanding the long-term implications of these interventions is crucial for developing effective strategies and tactics in future counterterrorism campaigns.

Challenges in Providing Assistance and Aid

In the battle against Al-Shabaab in Somalia, providing assistance and aid has been a daunting task for the United States military and its allies.

This subchapter delves into the various challenges encountered in the process.

One of the major obstacles faced in providing assistance and aid is the volatile security situation in Somalia. Al-Shabaab's presence and influence have created a hostile environment, making it difficult for military forces to operate effectively. The group's use of guerrilla warfare tactics, suicide bombings, and ambushes have resulted in casualties among both military personnel and civilians. This constant threat hampers the ability to establish stable supply lines and deliver aid to those in need.

Another significant challenge is the lack of infrastructure and resources in the country. Somalia has long been plagued by political instability and economic underdevelopment, which has hindered the provision of basic services to the population. The absence of proper roads, healthcare facilities, and educational institutions makes it challenging to deliver aid effectively. Additionally, the absence of a functioning government and the presence of corrupt officials have resulted in aid mismanagement and diversion, further hindering assistance efforts.

Cultural and linguistic barriers also pose challenges in providing aid. Somalia is a country with diverse ethnic groups and clans, each with its own customs and languages. This diversity makes it crucial to have a nuanced understanding of the local culture and traditions in order to effectively provide assistance. Failure to do so may lead to misunderstandings and further alienation of the local population, making it harder to win their trust and cooperation.

Furthermore, the ongoing conflict between different regional actors in Somalia adds complexity to the provision of assistance. The involvement of neighboring countries, such as Kenya and Ethiopia, in the fight against Al-Shabaab has led to competing interests and agendas. This has resulted in a lack of coordination and cooperation between these actors, making it challenging to develop a unified approach to providing aid.

In conclusion, the challenges in providing assistance and aid in the battle against Al-Shabaab in Somalia are numerous. The volatile security situation, lack of infrastructure, cultural barriers, and competing regional interests all contribute to the complexity of the task. Overcoming these challenges requires a comprehensive and coordinated approach, as well as a deep understanding of the local context and dynamics. Only through addressing these challenges can the United States military and its allies hope to make a meaningful impact in the fight against Al-Shabaab and bring stability and peace to Somalia.

Chapter 2: Analysis of the Effectiveness and Success of U.S. Efforts in Combating Al-Shabaab

Assessing the Impact of U.S. Military Interventions on Al-Shabaab's Strength and Influence

In the ongoing battle against Al-Shabaab, the United States has played a significant role in providing military interventions in Somalia. This subchapter aims to evaluate the impact of these interventions on Al-Shabaab's strength and influence, catering specifically to military historians and individuals interested in U.S. military interventions.

To fully comprehend the impact, it is imperative to delve into the history and background of U.S. military interventions in Somalia. Understanding the origins, ideology, and operations of Al-Shabaab within Somalia's complex political landscape is essential to gauge the effectiveness of U.S. efforts.

The U.S. has employed various counterterrorism strategies and tactics to combat Al-Shabaab. This subchapter will analyze these approaches, including drone strikes, training local forces, and intelligence sharing, to assess their effectiveness in weakening the extremist group's capabilities.

Moreover, the political landscape of Somalia has been significantly influenced by U.S. military interventions. It is crucial to evaluate the impact of these interventions on the country's governance and stability, considering the involvement of regional actors in the conflict.

While military interventions aim to combat extremism and provide security, they often come with humanitarian consequences and civilian casualties. This subchapter will address the ethical and legal considerations surrounding U.S. military interventions, shedding light on the challenges faced by the military in balancing security objectives with civilian protection.

To evaluate the effectiveness of U.S. efforts, a comprehensive analysis of the long-term implications of military interventions in Somalia is necessary. This includes assessing the extent to which Al-Shabaab has been weakened and analyzing the potential for the group to regroup or adapt in response to these interventions.

Furthermore, this subchapter will present a comparative analysis of U.S. military interventions in Somalia with other counterterrorism campaigns in the region. Drawing parallels and highlighting differences will provide valuable insights into the successes, failures, and lessons learned from these interventions.

In conclusion, assessing the impact of U.S. military interventions on Al-Shabaab's strength and influence is a complex task. This subchapter aims to provide military historians and those interested in U.S. military interventions with a comprehensive evaluation of the effectiveness, consequences, and long-term implications of these interventions in combating Al-Shabaab in Somalia. By analyzing the historical context, counterterrorism strategies, political landscape, and humanitarian considerations, this evaluation will contribute to a deeper understanding of the multifaceted dynamics of the conflict and inform future approaches to counterterrorism in the region.

Targeted Killings and Decapitation Strikes

One of the key strategies employed by the United States in its military interventions in Somalia to combat the extremist group Al-Shabaab has been targeted killings and decapitation strikes. These tactics involve identifying and eliminating high-value targets within the leadership structure of Al-Shabaab, with the aim of disrupting the group's operations and weakening its overall effectiveness.

Targeted killings and decapitation strikes have been a central component of U.S. counterterrorism efforts in Somalia due to the decentralized nature of Al-Shabaab's operations. Unlike traditional military organizations, Al-Shabaab does not have a clearly defined command structure, making it difficult to defeat through conventional means. By targeting key leaders, the United States aims to disrupt the group's ability to plan and execute attacks and create a leadership vacuum that hampers its ability to coordinate its activities.

These operations have primarily been carried out by special forces units, such as the Navy SEALs and the Army's Delta Force, who possess the necessary skills and expertise to conduct precision strikes. Intelligence plays a crucial role in identifying targets, with the United States relying on a wide range of sources, including human intelligence, signals intelligence, and surveillance technology, to gather information on the whereabouts and activities of high-value individuals within Al-Shabaab.

While targeted killings and decapitation strikes have been successful in eliminating some high-profile leaders of Al-Shabaab, their effectiveness in achieving long-term strategic objectives remains a subject of debate. Critics argue that these tactics can potentially result in the unintended consequences of radicalizing local populations and creating a cycle of violence and revenge. Additionally, the elimination of key leaders can lead to power struggles within Al-Shabaab, potentially enabling more radical elements to rise to prominence.

It is essential to evaluate the legal and ethical considerations surrounding targeted killings and decapitation strikes. These operations often take place in complex and fluid environments, where the distinction between combatants and civilians can be blurred. The

United States must ensure that its operations comply with international law, including the principles of proportionality and distinction, to minimize civilian casualties and collateral damage.

A comparative analysis of U.S. military interventions in Somalia with other counterterrorism campaigns in the region can provide valuable insights into the effectiveness and success of targeted killings and decapitation strikes. Understanding the similarities and differences between these operations can help inform future strategies and tactics in combating extremist groups in the Horn of Africa.

Overall, targeted killings and decapitation strikes have been an integral part of U.S. military interventions in Somalia to combat Al-Shabaab. While these tactics have achieved some short-term successes, their long-term effectiveness and potential consequences require further examination and evaluation. By critically analyzing their implementation and impact, military historians can contribute to a deeper understanding of the complexities involved in counterterrorism operations and inform future strategies in combating extremist groups.

Disruption of Al-Shabaab's Financing and Recruitment

One of the key challenges in combating the extremist group Al-Shabaab in Somalia has been its ability to sustain its operations through financing and recruitment. In this subchapter, we will examine the efforts made by the United States to disrupt Al-Shabaab's financing and recruitment networks, and evaluate their effectiveness in weakening the group.

Al-Shabaab has relied on a diverse range of funding sources, including taxation, extortion, and illicit activities such as charcoal smuggling and piracy. The United States has employed various strategies to disrupt these financial flows. One approach has been to work closely with international partners to monitor and interdict financial transactions linked to Al-Shabaab, targeting both domestic and international channels. This has involved cooperation with financial institutions, intelligence agencies, and law enforcement bodies to track and freeze the group's assets.

Another important aspect of disrupting Al-Shabaab's financing has been to address the underlying economic conditions that contribute to its resilience. The United States has supported programs aimed at promoting economic development and improving governance in Somalia, with the goal of reducing the socio-economic grievances that Al-Shabaab exploits for recruitment and support.

In terms of recruitment, Al-Shabaab has been successful in attracting disaffected youth by offering them a sense of purpose, belonging, and financial incentives. The United States has sought to counter this narrative by engaging with local communities and providing alternative opportunities for youth, such as education, vocational training, and job creation initiatives. Additionally, efforts have been made to counter Al-Shabaab's online propaganda and recruitment efforts through social media monitoring and counter-messaging campaigns.

While these efforts have had some success in disrupting Al-Shabaab's financing and recruitment networks, challenges remain. The group has proven resilient and adaptable, finding new ways to generate revenue and attract new members. Furthermore, the complex and dynamic nature of Somalia's political and security landscape has posed obstacles to sustained progress in this area.

In conclusion, disrupting Al-Shabaab's financing and recruitment networks is crucial for weakening the group and improving the security situation in Somalia. The United States has employed a range of strategies to address these challenges, including financial monitoring, economic development initiatives, and counter-messaging campaigns. While progress has been made, continued efforts and international cooperation will be necessary to further disrupt Al-Shabaab's ability to sustain itself and threaten regional stability.

Counterinsurgency Efforts and Support for Local Communities

In the battle against Al-Shabaab, U.S. military interventions in Somalia have focused on employing counterinsurgency strategies and providing support to local communities. These efforts have aimed to weaken the extremist group's hold on the region and enable the Somali government to regain control. This subchapter explores the significance and impact of these counterinsurgency efforts and the support provided to local communities.

Counterinsurgency efforts in Somalia have involved a multifaceted approach. The U.S. military has worked closely with the Somali government and regional actors to gather intelligence, conduct targeted operations, and disrupt Al-Shabaab's operations. By targeting key leaders and infrastructure, these efforts have aimed to degrade the group's capabilities and limit its ability to carry out attacks against both military and civilian targets.

Crucially, the U.S. military has recognized the importance of winning the hearts and minds of the local population. To this end, they have provided support to local communities in various forms. This support has included the provision of humanitarian aid, infrastructure development, and capacity building initiatives. By addressing the underlying socio-economic issues that contribute to the vulnerability of communities, the U.S. has sought to create an environment in which Al-Shabaab struggles to recruit and maintain support.

The impact of these counterinsurgency efforts and support for local communities has been significant. While Al-Shabaab remains a resilient and adaptive group, its control and influence have been significantly diminished. Through targeted strikes and disruption of its operations, the group's leadership has been weakened, leading to internal divisions and a loss of cohesion. Additionally, the provision of support to local communities has helped to build trust and foster cooperation between the Somali government, regional actors, and the population. This has created a more conducive environment for stability and reconstruction.

However, challenges remain. The complex nature of the conflict, coupled with Somalia's fragile political landscape, presents ongoing obstacles to achieving lasting success. Furthermore, the humanitarian consequences of military interventions and the potential for civilian casualties must be carefully considered and mitigated. Legal and ethical considerations surrounding these interventions are also important to address.

Comparisons with other counterterrorism campaigns in the region can provide valuable insights into the effectiveness and success of U.S. military interventions in Somalia. Evaluating the long-term implications of these interventions is crucial to understanding their overall impact on the region's security and stability.

In conclusion, counterinsurgency efforts and support for local communities have played a vital role in combating Al-Shabaab in Somalia. By employing a combination of targeted operations and humanitarian assistance, the U.S. military has sought to degrade the group's capabilities and win the support of the local population. While progress has been made, ongoing challenges and the need for careful evaluation should remain at the forefront of future interventions.

Evaluation of Counterterrorism Strategies and Tactics Employed by the U.S.

In the battle against the extremist group Al-Shabaab in Somalia, the United States has employed various counterterrorism strategies and tactics. This subchapter aims to evaluate the effectiveness and success of these efforts, while also considering the historical, political, and humanitarian implications of U.S. military interventions.

To understand the context of U.S. military interventions in Somalia, it is essential to explore the history and background of these interventions. The origins, ideology, and operations of Al-Shabaab within Somalia provide crucial insights into the group's motivations and capabilities.

The U.S. has implemented a range of counterterrorism strategies and tactics to combat Al-Shabaab. These include direct military action, intelligence sharing, training and equipping local forces, and engaging in diplomatic efforts. By analyzing the impact of these strategies on the political landscape in Somalia, we can assess their effectiveness in weakening or dismantling Al-Shabaab's influence.

However, it is important to acknowledge the humanitarian consequences and civilian casualties resulting from U.S. military interventions. By examining these factors, we can better understand the ethical and legal considerations surrounding U.S. actions in Somalia.

Additionally, this subchapter will explore the role and involvement of regional actors in U.S. military interventions. Understanding the dynamics between the U.S., Somalia, and neighboring countries provides insights into the complexities of counterterrorism operations in the region.

By comparing U.S. military interventions in Somalia with other counterterrorism campaigns in the region, we can gain a broader perspective on the successes and failures of U.S. strategies and tactics. This analysis will allow military historians to draw lessons and identify best practices for future counterterrorism efforts.

Finally, assessing the long-term implications of U.S. military interventions will help determine the lasting effects on Somalia's stability and security. This evaluation will consider not only the immediate impact on Al-Shabaab but also the potential for future extremism and political instability.

In conclusion, this subchapter provides a comprehensive evaluation of the counterterrorism strategies and tactics employed by the U.S. in Somalia. By delving into the historical, political, and humanitarian dimensions of these interventions, military historians can gain valuable insights into the effectiveness and long-term implications of U.S. efforts in combating Al-Shabaab.

Strengths and Weaknesses of Direct Military Action

In the ongoing battle against Al-Shabaab in Somalia, direct military action has been a key strategy employed by the United States. This subchapter examines the strengths and weaknesses of this approach, providing military historians with a comprehensive evaluation of its effectiveness.

One of the primary strengths of direct military action is its ability to swiftly neutralize immediate threats posed by Al-Shabaab. Through targeted airstrikes, raids, and special operations, the U.S. military has been successful in eliminating key leaders and disrupting the group's operations. This approach has proven effective in degrading Al-Shabaab's capabilities and reducing its overall strength.

Another strength is the ability of direct military action to provide a clear and decisive message to Al-Shabaab and other extremist groups. By demonstrating a willingness to use force, the United States sends a strong signal that terrorism will not be tolerated. This can deter potential recruits and weaken the group's support base.

However, there are also inherent weaknesses associated with direct military action. One of the main challenges is the risk of civilian casualties and collateral damage. Despite efforts to minimize harm, the use of explosives and advanced weaponry increases the likelihood of unintended harm to non-combatants. This can undermine local support for U.S. military interventions and fuel anti-American sentiment.

Furthermore, direct military action alone may not address the root causes of extremism. While it can disrupt Al-Shabaab's operations, it does little to address the underlying grievances that fuel the group's recruitment and support. This necessitates a comprehensive approach that combines military action with diplomatic, economic, and developmental efforts to address the socio-political conditions that allow extremism to thrive.

Additionally, the sustainability of direct military action is a concern. The use of force requires significant resources, both in terms of manpower and financial investment. Overreliance on military interventions can strain resources and divert attention away from other pressing national security priorities.

In conclusion, direct military action has its strengths and weaknesses in the fight against Al-Shabaab in Somalia. While it can provide immediate results in neutralizing threats and sending a strong message, it also carries the risk of civilian casualties and may not address the root causes of extremism. Military historians must carefully evaluate the effectiveness of this approach in order to inform future counterterrorism strategies and ensure a comprehensive and sustainable approach to combating extremist groups.

Effectiveness of Supporting Local Security Forces

One of the key strategies employed by the United States in its military interventions in Somalia to combat the extremist group Al-Shabaab has been the support and training of local security forces. This subchapter aims to evaluate the effectiveness of this approach and its impact on the overall mission.

Supporting local security forces has been a central pillar of the U.S. counterterrorism strategy in Somalia. By empowering and equipping local forces, the goal is to build their capacity to independently tackle the threat posed by Al-Shabaab, while also reducing the need for direct U.S. military involvement. This approach aligns with the broader objective of fostering stability and security in Somalia, as well as ensuring the long-term sustainability of counterterrorism efforts.

However, the effectiveness of supporting local security forces in Somalia has been mixed. On one hand, there have been instances where the U.S.-trained Somali security forces have shown commendable progress in their ability to combat Al-Shabaab. They have successfully conducted joint operations with U.S. troops, leading to the capture or elimination of high-value targets within the extremist group. These successes demonstrate the positive impact of investing in local forces and building their capacity.

On the other hand, challenges persist. The Somali security forces often face issues such as corruption, inadequate resources, and a lack of coordination. This hampers their ability to effectively counter Al-Shabaab and maintain stability within the country. Additionally, there have been reports of human rights abuses committed by some of these forces, raising concerns about the long-term sustainability of their efforts.

It is crucial to recognize the complex nature of supporting local security forces in Somalia. The success or failure of this approach is dependent on various factors, including the level of political will, the availability of resources, and the commitment to addressing structural issues within the security forces.

In conclusion, while supporting local security forces is an essential component of U.S. military interventions in Somalia to combat Al-Shabaab, its effectiveness has been a mixed bag. While there have been notable successes, challenges and limitations persist. To ensure the long-term success of this strategy, it is crucial to address the underlying issues within the Somali security forces and provide sustained support in terms of training, resources, and oversight. Only then can the local forces play a more significant role in countering Al-Shabaab and achieving stability in Somalia.

Role of Intelligence and Surveillance in Countering Al-Shabaab

The Role of Intelligence and Surveillance in Countering Al-Shabaab

Intelligence and surveillance play a crucial role in countering the extremist group Al-Shabaab in Somalia. As military historians, it is essential to evaluate the significance of these tools in the context of U.S. military interventions in the fight against Al-Shabaab.

Intelligence gathering is the backbone of any successful counterterrorism operation. It involves collecting, analyzing, and disseminating information to support decision-making and operational planning. In the case of Al-Shabaab, intelligence is critical to understanding the group's origins, ideology, and operational capabilities. By acquiring this knowledge, U.S. forces can effectively target and disrupt Al-Shabaab's activities.

Surveillance complements intelligence by providing real-time information on the ground. Through aerial reconnaissance, electronic monitoring, and other surveillance methods, the U.S. military can monitor Al-Shabaab's movements, identify high-value targets, and gather evidence for future operations. The ability to track and locate

Al-Shabaab fighters and leaders is instrumental in preventing attacks and dismantling their networks.

Additionally, intelligence and surveillance enable the U.S. military to develop a comprehensive understanding of the political landscape in Somalia. By monitoring key actors and factions, the U.S. can identify potential allies, assess the impact of its interventions, and mitigate any unintended consequences. This knowledge is crucial for ensuring that U.S. efforts align with the broader political objectives in the region.

Furthermore, intelligence and surveillance help minimize civilian casualties and humanitarian consequences. By accurately identifying Al-Shabaab fighters and distinguishing them from innocent civilians, the U.S. military can limit collateral damage. This not only reflects the ethical considerations surrounding military interventions but also prevents the radicalization of the local population.

The role of regional actors in U.S. military interventions should also be considered. Intelligence sharing and coordination with regional partners, such as the African Union Mission in Somalia (AMISOM), enhance the effectiveness of counterterrorism operations. Regional actors possess local knowledge and networks, which can significantly contribute to intelligence gathering efforts.

In conclusion, intelligence and surveillance are indispensable in countering Al-Shabaab in Somalia. These tools enable the U.S. military to gather vital information, monitor the group's activities, and make informed decisions. By leveraging intelligence and surveillance effectively, the U.S. can maximize its efforts in combating Al-Shabaab while minimizing civilian casualties and humanitarian consequences. Understanding the role of these tools is essential for evaluating the effectiveness and success of U.S. military interventions in Somalia.

Role and Involvement of Regional Actors in U.S. Military Interventions

The role and involvement of regional actors in U.S. military interventions in Somalia have played a significant role in shaping the outcomes and effectiveness of these operations. Regional actors have been crucial in providing support, intelligence, and resources to the United States, as well as contributing to the overall stability and security of the region. This subchapter evaluates the impact and contributions of these regional actors in the fight against the extremist group Al-Shabaab.

One of the key regional actors involved in U.S. military interventions in Somalia is the African Union Mission in Somalia (AMISOM). AMISOM, comprised of troops from various African countries, has been instrumental in supporting the Somali government in its efforts to combat Al-Shabaab. The presence of AMISOM forces has helped to stabilize the country and create an environment conducive to the success of U.S. counterterrorism strategies. Their contribution in terms of troops, equipment, and expertise has bolstered the effectiveness of U.S. operations against Al-Shabaab.

Another important regional actor is Kenya, which has been actively involved in the fight against Al-Shabaab. Kenya has deployed its military forces into Somalia, conducting cross-border operations to disrupt and degrade the capabilities of the extremist group. The Kenyan military has been instrumental in undermining Al-Shabaab's operational capabilities, limiting its ability to launch attacks both within Somalia and in neighboring countries.

Ethiopia has also played a significant role in U.S. military interventions in Somalia. Ethiopian forces have been deployed to support the Somali government and counter Al-Shabaab's influence. Ethiopian troops have conducted joint operations with U.S. forces, targeting high-value Al-Shabaab leaders and disrupting the group's operations.

In addition to these regional actors, other countries in the region, such as Djibouti and Uganda, have also contributed troops and resources to the fight against Al-Shabaab. Their involvement has further enhanced the effectiveness of U.S. military interventions, providing a broader regional approach to countering the extremist group.

The involvement of regional actors in U.S. military interventions in Somalia has not only been crucial in terms of military support but has also had significant political and diplomatic implications. The cooperation and coordination between these regional actors and the United States have helped to strengthen relationships and build trust, fostering a unified approach to tackling the threat of Al-Shabaab.

Overall, the role and involvement of regional actors in U.S. military interventions in Somalia have been essential in achieving success against Al-Shabaab. The combined efforts of these actors, along with the United States, have significantly degraded the capabilities of the extremist group and have contributed to the overall stability and security of the region. The evaluation of their contributions provides valuable insights for military historians and allows for a comprehensive understanding of the complex dynamics involved in conducting military interventions in the fight against extremist groups like Al-Shabaab.

African Union Mission in Somalia (AMISOM)

The African Union Mission in Somalia (AMISOM) has played a crucial role in the fight against the extremist group Al-Shabaab in Somalia. As military historians, it is important to evaluate the effectiveness and impact of AMISOM's involvement in the context of U.S. military interventions in Somalia to combat Al-Shabaab.

AMISOM was established in 2007 by the African Union with the mandate to support the Federal Government of Somalia in its efforts to stabilize the country and combat Al-Shabaab. The mission has been authorized and supported by the United Nations Security Council, demonstrating the international community's recognition of the threat posed by Al-Shabaab.

The origins of Al-Shabaab can be traced back to the early 2000s when it emerged as the youth wing of the Islamic Courts Union (ICU), a group that aimed to establish Sharia law in Somalia. Over time, Al-Shabaab became increasingly radicalized and engaged in acts of terrorism, including suicide bombings, assassinations, and attacks on African Union and Somali government forces.

U.S. counterterrorism strategies and tactics have been employed in collaboration with AMISOM to degrade and defeat Al-Shabaab. These efforts have included targeted airstrikes, drone surveillance, and training and equipping Somali security forces. However, it is important to assess the long-term implications of these interventions, considering the complex political landscape in Somalia.

While AMISOM and U.S. military interventions have made significant strides in weakening Al-Shabaab, there have also been humanitarian consequences and civilian casualties. The indiscriminate nature of Al-Shabaab's attacks and the complexity of the conflict have resulted in unintended harm to innocent civilians. It is crucial to analyze the ethical considerations surrounding these interventions and seek to minimize civilian harm in future operations.

Regional actors, such as Kenya and Ethiopia, have also played a role in U.S. military interventions in Somalia. Their involvement has both positive and negative implications, as they bring additional resources and expertise but also have their own political and strategic interests in the region.

To evaluate the effectiveness and success of U.S. efforts in combating Al-Shabaab, it is important to compare these interventions with other counterterrorism campaigns in the region. Lessons can be learned from previous interventions in Afghanistan and Iraq to inform future strategies in Somalia.

In conclusion, AMISOM's involvement in the fight against Al-Shabaab has been instrumental in stabilizing Somalia and weakening the extremist group. However, the long-term implications, ethical considerations, and regional dynamics must be carefully evaluated to ensure a sustainable and effective approach in combating terrorism in the region.

Kenya's Involvement in Somalia

Kenya's involvement in Somalia has been a crucial element in the fight against the extremist group Al-Shabaab. As military historians, it is essential to analyze and evaluate the impact of Kenya's interventions in Somalia, specifically in the context of the broader U.S. military efforts against Al-Shabaab.

Kenya's involvement in Somalia can be traced back to October 2011 when it launched Operation Linda Nchi (Protect the Nation) in response to increasing threats and attacks from Al-Shabaab. The primary objective of this intervention was to create a buffer zone along the Kenya-Somalia border and prevent further infiltration of Al-Shabaab militants into Kenyan territory. Kenya's military operations were further reinforced by its participation in the African Union Mission in Somalia (AMISOM), which aimed to stabilize Somalia and weaken Al-Shabaab's influence.

Kenya's strategic location and historical ties with Somalia make it a critical regional actor in combating Al-Shabaab. Its involvement in Somalia has not only been military but also economic and political.

Kenya has provided humanitarian assistance and accommodated a significant number of Somali refugees, which has had both positive and negative consequences for its own security and stability.

The effectiveness of Kenya's military interventions in Somalia can be assessed by analyzing the impact on Al-Shabaab's operations and territorial control. Kenya's interventions, along with those of other AMISOM troops, have successfully pushed Al-Shabaab out of major cities and disrupted its operations. However, Al-Shabaab remains a persistent threat, capable of carrying out asymmetric attacks and regrouping in rural areas.

The long-term implications of Kenya's involvement in Somalia are multifaceted. On one hand, it has contributed to the weakening of Al-Shabaab and the gradual restoration of stability in Somalia. On the other hand, the interventions have had significant humanitarian consequences, including civilian casualties and displacement.

The legal and ethical considerations surrounding Kenya's interventions in Somalia are crucial to evaluate. The interventions have raised questions about the extent of Kenya's self-defense, the protection of civilian lives, and adherence to international humanitarian law.

Comparisons can be drawn between Kenya's interventions in Somalia and other counterterrorism campaigns in the region, such as the U.S. interventions in Afghanistan and Iraq. By examining similarities and differences, military historians can gain a broader understanding of the challenges and successes faced in combating extremist groups in different contexts.

In conclusion, Kenya's involvement in Somalia has played a pivotal role in the fight against Al-Shabaab. By evaluating the history, impact, effectiveness, and long-term implications of Kenya's interventions, military historians can contribute to a comprehensive understanding of the broader U.S. military efforts in Somalia and the region as a whole.

Ethiopia's Role in Combating Al-Shabaab

Ethiopia has played a significant role in the fight against the extremist group Al-Shabaab in Somalia. As one of the key regional actors involved in U.S. military interventions, Ethiopia's contributions have had a profound impact on the overall dynamics of the conflict.

Historically, Ethiopia has had a complex relationship with Somalia. The two countries share a long border and have often found themselves on opposing sides of various conflicts. However, when it comes to combating Al-Shabaab, Ethiopia and Somalia have found common ground.

Ethiopia first intervened militarily in Somalia in 2006, as part of the U.S.-backed African Union Mission in Somalia (AMISOM). This intervention aimed to stabilize the country and weaken Al-Shabaab's grip on power. Ethiopian forces, in collaboration with other AMISOM troops, successfully pushed back Al-Shabaab from major urban centers, including the capital, Mogadishu.

Ethiopia's involvement in Somalia has not been without controversy. While their military operations have had some success in countering Al-Shabaab, there have been reports of civilian casualties and allegations of human rights abuses. These allegations highlight the importance of conducting military interventions with a strong focus on protecting civilian lives and upholding international humanitarian laws.

Ethiopia's role in combating Al-Shabaab extends beyond military operations. The country has been actively involved in providing diplomatic support to the Somali government, as well as offering training and capacity-building assistance to the Somali National Army.

Ethiopia's experience in counterterrorism and its knowledge of the region have been instrumental in shaping U.S. military strategies.

Furthermore, Ethiopia's involvement has had significant implications for the political landscape in Somalia. It has helped to strengthen the Somali government's position and weaken Al-Shabaab's influence. However, challenges remain, as the group continues to carry out attacks and maintain a presence in rural areas.

In conclusion, Ethiopia's role in combating Al-Shabaab in Somalia has been crucial in the overall fight against this extremist group. Their military interventions, diplomatic support, and capacity-building efforts have contributed to the weakening of Al-Shabaab and the stabilization of Somalia. However, it is essential to assess the long-term implications of these interventions and address any humanitarian consequences and civilian casualties. Additionally, the legal and ethical considerations surrounding military interventions must be carefully evaluated to ensure the protection of human rights. Comparisons with other counterterrorism campaigns in the region can provide valuable insights into the effectiveness and success of U.S. military interventions in Somalia.

Chapter 3: Assessing the Long-Term Implications of U.S. Military Interventions in Somalia

Impact on Regional Stability and Security

The impact of U.S. military interventions in Somalia on regional stability and security has been a topic of great significance and concern. As military historians delve into the evaluation of U.S. interventions in the fight against the extremist group Al-Shabaab, it is crucial to examine the wider implications on the political landscape and the overall stability of the region.

The history and background of U.S. military interventions in Somalia provide essential context for understanding the subsequent impact on regional stability. From the ill-fated Operation Gothic Serpent in 1993 to more recent efforts, such as Operation Odyssey Lightning in 2016, the United States has sought to combat the threat posed by Al-Shabaab through a variety of strategies and tactics.

Al-Shabaab's origins, ideology, and operations within Somalia have had far-reaching consequences for regional stability. The group's ability to exploit political instability and ungoverned spaces in Somalia has created a breeding ground for extremism, posing a significant threat to neighboring countries, including Kenya and Ethiopia. U.S. interventions, therefore, aim to not only address the immediate security concerns in Somalia but also mitigate the spillover effects on the region.

The effectiveness and success of U.S. efforts in combating Al-Shabaab must be critically analyzed to understand their impact on regional stability. Assessing the long-term implications of these interventions requires a comprehensive examination of the evolving nature of the conflict and the role of regional actors. The involvement of countries like Kenya and Ethiopia, both in military operations and in supporting the Federal Government of Somalia, has shaped the dynamics of the conflict and influenced the overall stability of the region.

It is crucial to consider the legal and ethical considerations surrounding U.S. military interventions. The protection of civilian lives and adherence to international human rights standards are of utmost importance. Assessing the humanitarian consequences and civilian casualties resulting from U.S. interventions is essential to understanding the broader impact on regional stability and security.

Comparisons with other counterterrorism campaigns in the region, such as the fight against Boko Haram in Nigeria or the Islamic State in the Sahel, can provide valuable insights into the effectiveness of U.S. interventions in Somalia. By examining the similarities and differences, military historians can identify best practices and lessons learned that can inform future interventions.

In conclusion, the impact of U.S. military interventions in Somalia on regional stability and security cannot be underestimated. Understanding the complex interplay between political dynamics, regional actors, and the evolving nature of the conflict is essential for military historians evaluating the effectiveness and success of these interventions. By considering the humanitarian consequences, legal and ethical considerations, and comparing with other counterterrorism campaigns, a comprehensive assessment can be made to inform future endeavors in combating extremism in the region.

Spillover Effects of Conflict and Instability

In the battle against the extremist group Al-Shabaab, the United States has engaged in multiple military interventions in Somalia. These interventions have had far-reaching consequences, not only within

Somalia but also in the wider region. This subchapter delves into the spillover effects of conflict and instability resulting from these interventions, offering valuable insights for military historians.

One key aspect to consider is the impact of U.S. military interventions on the political landscape in Somalia. These interventions have often been seen as a necessary response to the threat of Al-Shabaab, but they have also had unintended consequences. The interventions have at times bolstered certain factions or leaders, creating a dependency on external forces and undermining local governance structures. Understanding these dynamics is crucial for evaluating the long-term stability and effectiveness of U.S. interventions.

Another critical dimension is the humanitarian consequences and civilian casualties resulting from U.S. military interventions. While the primary objective is to combat Al-Shabaab, the use of airstrikes and other military tactics can inadvertently harm innocent civilians and exacerbate the humanitarian crisis. Assessing the ethical implications of these interventions is essential for understanding the broader context in which they occur.

Additionally, it is crucial to analyze the effectiveness and success of U.S. efforts in combating Al-Shabaab. While these interventions have dealt significant blows to the group, they have not eradicated the threat entirely. Understanding the reasons behind this limited success can shed light on the complexities of counterterrorism strategies and tactics employed against Al-Shabaab, as well as provide lessons for future operations.

Moreover, the role and involvement of regional actors in U.S. military interventions cannot be overlooked. Somalia's neighbors, such as Kenya and Ethiopia, have played a significant role in supporting U.S. efforts. Evaluating the extent of their involvement and the implications for regional stability is crucial for understanding the broader dynamics at play.

Finally, this subchapter also explores the legal and ethical considerations surrounding U.S. military interventions. The use of force and the potential violation of international law raise important questions about the legitimacy and accountability of these interventions. Comparisons with other counterterrorism campaigns in the region can provide valuable insights into the unique challenges faced in Somalia.

In conclusion, examining the spillover effects of conflict and instability resulting from U.S. military interventions in Somalia is vital for military historians. It provides a comprehensive understanding of the broader implications of these interventions, including their impact on the political landscape, humanitarian consequences, effectiveness, regional dynamics, and legal and ethical considerations. By evaluating these factors, military historians can contribute to a more nuanced understanding of the battle against Al-Shabaab and inform future military interventions and counterterrorism strategies.

Al-Shabaab's Transnational Connections and Influence

The subchapter on "Al-Shabaab's Transnational Connections and Influence" delves into the complex web of international relationships and influences that have shaped the rise and expansion of Al-Shabaab in Somalia. This section provides military historians with a comprehensive understanding of the group's transnational connections and the implications they have had on U.S. military interventions in Somalia.

Al-Shabaab, an extremist group with origins in the early 2000s, has evolved from a local insurgency to a transnational threat with global aspirations. This subchapter explores the ideological foundations of

Al-Shabaab and its origins as a radical offshoot of the Islamic Courts Union (ICU). It examines the group's ties to international terrorist organizations, such as Al-Qaeda, and their impact on shaping Al-Shabaab's goals, strategies, and tactics.

Furthermore, this section analyzes the various transnational connections that have facilitated Al-Shabaab's growth and influence. It highlights the group's recruitment networks, funding sources, and arms smuggling routes, which span across the Horn of Africa and beyond. These connections have allowed Al-Shabaab to sustain its operations and maintain a resilient presence despite military interventions by the United States and other regional actors.

The subchapter also evaluates the role and involvement of regional actors in supporting or countering Al-Shabaab. It examines the contributions of neighboring countries, such as Kenya and Ethiopia, as well as international organizations like the African Union Mission in Somalia (AMISOM), in combating the group. By understanding these regional dynamics, military historians can assess the effectiveness of U.S. military interventions in Somalia and identify areas for improvement.

Additionally, this section addresses the implications of Al-Shabaab's transnational connections on the political landscape in Somalia. It examines how the group's influence has affected the stability and governance of the country, particularly in areas under its control. The subchapter also explores the humanitarian consequences and civilian casualties resulting from U.S. military interventions, shedding light on the ethical considerations surrounding such operations.

Finally, this section offers a comparative analysis of U.S. military interventions in Somalia with other counterterrorism campaigns in the region. By examining similarities and differences between these campaigns, military historians can gain insights into the long-term implications of U.S. interventions and identify best practices for future operations.

In conclusion, the subchapter on "Al-Shabaab's Transnational Connections and Influence" provides military historians with a comprehensive analysis of the group's international relationships and the impact they have had on U.S. military interventions in Somalia. By understanding these connections, historians can evaluate the effectiveness of past interventions and inform future strategies to combat extremist groups in the region.

Effects on Local Communities and Civil Society

The impact of U.S. military interventions in Somalia to combat the extremist group Al-Shabaab extends far beyond the battlefield. This subchapter explores the effects on local communities and civil society, shedding light on the complex dynamics that have shaped the Somali landscape.

One of the key aspects to consider is the history and background of U.S. military interventions in Somalia. Understanding the context in which these interventions took place allows for a more comprehensive analysis of their consequences. From the early 1990s to the present day, the United States has been involved in various operations seeking to counter the rise of Al-Shabaab and stabilize the country.

Al-Shabaab's origins, ideology, and operations in Somalia play a crucial role in shaping the impact of U.S. interventions. This subchapter delves into the group's evolution and explores the tactics employed by Al-Shabaab to maintain control and expand its influence. It also examines the ways in which U.S. counterterrorism strategies and tactics have adapted over time to counter these threats.

While the goal of U.S. military interventions is to combat Al-Shabaab, the impact on the political landscape in Somalia cannot be ignored.

The subchapter examines how these interventions have shaped political dynamics within the country and the wider region. It explores the role and involvement of regional actors, such as the African Union Mission in Somalia (AMISOM), and assesses the long-term implications of their collaboration with the United States.

However, it is essential to acknowledge the humanitarian consequences and civilian casualties that have resulted from U.S. military interventions. This subchapter discusses the ethical considerations surrounding these interventions, including the responsibility to protect civilian populations and mitigate harm.

To evaluate the effectiveness and success of U.S. efforts in combating Al-Shabaab, a comprehensive analysis of the impact on local communities and civil society is necessary. This subchapter examines the social and economic consequences of these interventions, exploring the ways in which they have affected livelihoods, education, and healthcare.

In comparing U.S. military interventions in Somalia with other counterterrorism campaigns in the region, this subchapter provides military historians with a broader perspective. By considering the similarities and differences, it becomes possible to draw valuable lessons and insights for future operations.

In conclusion, the effects of U.S. military interventions in Somalia extend beyond the military realm. This subchapter addresses the impact on local communities and civil society, considering the humanitarian, political, and socio-economic consequences. By analyzing these effects, military historians can gain a deeper understanding of the complex dynamics at play in the fight against Al-Shabaab and the challenges of counterterrorism operations in the region.

Community Perceptions of U.S. Military Interventions

One critical aspect to consider when evaluating U.S. military interventions in Somalia is the community perceptions of these operations. The local population's attitudes and beliefs towards the presence and actions of American forces can significantly impact the success or failure of military objectives, as well as the long-term stability and political landscape of the country.

Historically, U.S. military interventions in Somalia have been met with mixed reactions from the local communities. While some segments of the population appreciate the international support in countering the extremist group Al-Shabaab, others view the presence of foreign troops as an infringement on their sovereignty and a violation of their cultural values.

Understanding the origins, ideology, and operations of Al-Shabaab is crucial in comprehending community perceptions. Al-Shabaab emerged as an extremist group with the aim of establishing a strict Islamic state in Somalia. Their brutal tactics and attacks on civilians have bred fear and resentment among the population. Consequently, some communities may view U.S. military interventions as necessary evils, while others may perceive them as a catalyst for further violence and radicalization.

The effectiveness and success of U.S. efforts in combating Al-Shabaab must be evaluated through the lens of community perceptions. It is essential to consider whether military interventions have succeeded in gaining the trust and cooperation of local communities, or if they have inadvertently alienated and radicalized segments of the population. The impact on the political landscape in Somalia is closely tied to these community perceptions. If the local population perceives the U.S. military interventions as illegitimate or ineffective, it can undermine the legitimacy of the Somali government and create fertile ground for extremist groups to exploit.

Moreover, the humanitarian consequences and civilian casualties resulting from U.S. military interventions cannot be ignored. While the primary objective is to neutralize Al-Shabaab, collateral damage and civilian casualties can fuel anti-American sentiments and undermine the perception of the U.S. as a force for stability and security in the region.

Analyzing the involvement of regional actors in U.S. military interventions is also crucial. Regional actors, such as neighboring countries and international organizations, play a significant role in shaping community perceptions of these interventions. Their support and cooperation can enhance the legitimacy and effectiveness of U.S. military actions, while their opposition can fuel skepticism and resistance among the local population.

In conclusion, community perceptions of U.S. military interventions in Somalia are vital in understanding the effectiveness, success, and long-term implications of these operations. The way in which local communities perceive the presence and actions of American forces can significantly impact the political landscape, cooperation, and stability in the country. Evaluating community perceptions also involves examining the humanitarian consequences, civilian casualties, and the role of regional actors in shaping these perceptions. By considering these factors, military historians can gain a comprehensive understanding of the complexities surrounding U.S. military interventions and their impact on Somalia's fight against Al-Shabaab.

Empowerment or Marginalization of Local Actors

The subchapter "Empowerment or Marginalization of Local Actors" delves into the complex dynamics between the United States military interventions in Somalia and the role of local actors in combating the extremist group Al-Shabaab. This section aims to provide military historians with a comprehensive analysis of how these interventions have impacted the empowerment or marginalization of local actors.

Throughout the history of U.S. military interventions in Somalia, there have been instances where local actors have been empowered, while in other cases, they have been marginalized. The effectiveness and success of these interventions heavily depend on the level of engagement and collaboration with local actors.

On one hand, the United States has recognized the importance of partnering with local forces and empowering them to take a leading role in combating Al-Shabaab. This approach has been evident through the establishment of training programs and the provision of military equipment to the Somali National Army and African Union Mission in Somalia (AMISOM). By empowering these local actors, the U.S. aims to build their capacity to independently tackle the extremist threat.

However, there have also been instances where the U.S. interventions have inadvertently marginalized local actors. This has been primarily due to the reliance on direct military operations, such as drone strikes and special forces raids, which bypass local authorities and communities. These actions can create a sense of resentment among the local population, further fueling grievances that Al-Shabaab exploits to gain support.

Furthermore, the involvement of regional actors in U.S. military interventions in Somalia adds another layer of complexity to the empowerment or marginalization of local actors. Regional actors, such as Kenya and Ethiopia, have pursued their own national interests in Somalia, often at the expense of local actors. This has resulted in power struggles, competing agendas, and limited local ownership of the counterterrorism efforts.

It is crucial for military historians to assess the long-term implications of these interventions on the empowerment or marginalization of local actors. By understanding the impact on the political landscape, humanitarian consequences, and civilian casualties, historians can evaluate the effectiveness and ethical considerations surrounding U.S. military interventions.

Ultimately, comparing U.S. military interventions in Somalia with other counterterrorism campaigns in the region provides a broader perspective to understand the unique challenges faced in Somalia and the importance of empowering local actors. By striking a balance between empowering local actors and employing effective counterterrorism strategies, the United States can contribute to a sustainable and locally-led solution to combat Al-Shabaab in Somalia.

Evaluating Progress in Achieving Long-Term Stability and Peace in Somalia

Introduction:

The subchapter "Evaluating Progress in Achieving Long-Term Stability and Peace in Somalia" critically examines the outcomes and effectiveness of U.S. military interventions in combating the extremist group Al-Shabaab. This evaluation is crucial for military historians studying the history and impact of U.S. military interventions in Somalia to combat Al-Shabaab. By analyzing the long-term implications, political landscape, humanitarian consequences, and regional involvement, this subchapter provides a comprehensive assessment of the progress made in achieving stability and peace in Somalia.

Assessing Progress:

To evaluate the progress made in achieving long-term stability and peace in Somalia, it is essential to consider the impact of U.S. counterterrorism strategies and tactics against Al-Shabaab. The chapter delves into an analysis of the effectiveness and success of these efforts, examining the extent to which Al-Shabaab's origins, ideology, and operations have been curtailed.

Furthermore, the subchapter evaluates the role and involvement of regional actors in U.S. military interventions. Understanding the dynamics and contributions of neighboring countries and regional organizations is crucial to comprehending the broader context in which stability and peace in Somalia are pursued.

Additionally, the subchapter explores the impact of U.S. military interventions on the political landscape in Somalia. The evaluation takes into account the changes in governance, state-building efforts, and the role of local actors in shaping the trajectory of stability and peace.

Humanitarian Consequences and Ethical Considerations:

An integral part of the evaluation involves assessing the humanitarian consequences and civilian casualties resulting from U.S. military interventions. By examining the unintended consequences and ethical considerations surrounding these interventions, military historians gain a deeper understanding of the complexities associated with counterterrorism campaigns.

Comparative Analysis:

To provide a comprehensive evaluation, the subchapter also compares U.S. military interventions in Somalia with other counterterrorism campaigns in the region. By examining similarities and differences in approach, strategy, and outcomes, military historians can draw valuable insights and lessons from these comparative analyses.

Conclusion:

The subchapter "Evaluating Progress in Achieving Long-Term Stability and Peace in Somalia" offers a comprehensive evaluation of U.S. military interventions in the fight against Al-Shabaab. The assessment considers various factors, including the effectiveness of counterterrorism strategies, regional involvement, political landscape changes, humanitarian consequences, and ethical considerations. By critically analyzing these aspects, military historians gain a nuanced understanding of the progress made in achieving stability and peace in Somalia and the long-term implications of U.S. military interventions.

Political Reconciliation and State-Building Efforts

In the complex battle against the extremist group Al-Shabaab in Somalia, it becomes imperative to evaluate the role of political reconciliation and state-building efforts. This subchapter will delve into the impact and effectiveness of such initiatives undertaken by the United States military in combating Al-Shabaab.

Political reconciliation aims to bring together various factions and stakeholders within Somalia's political landscape to foster stability and unity. State-building efforts, on the other hand, focus on establishing functioning institutions and governance structures to rebuild and strengthen the Somali state. These two interrelated processes are crucial in countering Al-Shabaab's influence and addressing the root causes of extremism.

The United States military interventions in Somalia have recognized the importance of political reconciliation and state-building. By supporting and collaborating with Somali government institutions, the U.S. has sought to enhance their capacity to govern effectively and provide security for their citizens. This has involved training and equipping Somali security forces, as well as providing advisory support to political leaders.

However, the challenges of political reconciliation and state-building in Somalia are immense. The country has been plagued by decades of conflict, clan rivalries, and weak governance. These factors have created a fertile ground for Al-Shabaab's recruitment and operations. The United States' efforts to promote political reconciliation and state-building have faced obstacles such as corruption, lack of trust among clans, and limited resources.

Furthermore, the success of political reconciliation and state-building efforts is closely tied to the broader regional dynamics. The involvement of regional actors, such as neighboring countries and the African Union, has both positive and negative implications. While regional cooperation can provide vital support, it also introduces complexities and competing interests.

Assessing the long-term implications of U.S. military interventions in Somalia requires considering the sustainability of political reconciliation and state-building efforts. These initiatives cannot be limited to short-term military engagements but must be accompanied by comprehensive strategies for economic development, justice, and social cohesion. Moreover, legal and ethical considerations surrounding U.S. military interventions must be examined, such as adherence to international humanitarian law and minimizing civilian casualties.

Comparing U.S. military interventions in Somalia with other counterterrorism campaigns in the region allows for a broader perspective on the challenges and successes. By analyzing the strategies and tactics employed, as well as the humanitarian consequences, it becomes possible to draw valuable lessons and identify best practices for future interventions in the fight against extremism.

Ultimately, political reconciliation and state-building efforts are critical components in the battle against Al-Shabaab in Somalia. The evaluation of U.S. military interventions in this context provides valuable insights into the complexities and effectiveness of such initiatives. By understanding the dynamics of political reconciliation, state-building, and their impact on countering extremism, military historians can contribute to developing more comprehensive and sustainable approaches for future operations.

Addressing Root Causes of Extremism and Radicalization

In the battle against Al-Shabaab, it is crucial to address the root causes of extremism and radicalization in Somalia. While military interventions play a significant role in combating this extremist group, they alone cannot eradicate the problem. To truly make a sustainable impact, it is imperative to understand and address the underlying factors that contribute to the rise of Al-Shabaab.

One of the key factors behind Al-Shabaab's emergence is the deep-rooted political instability in Somalia. The country has been plagued by decades of civil war, weak governance, and a lack of effective institutions. This environment provides fertile ground for extremist ideologies to take hold and recruit disillusioned individuals. Therefore, to counter Al-Shabaab effectively, efforts should focus on strengthening political institutions and promoting stability.

Another critical factor contributing to radicalization is the lack of economic opportunities for the Somali population. High levels of poverty and unemployment create a sense of hopelessness among the youth, making them susceptible to extremist ideologies. Investing in economic development, job creation, and vocational training programs can provide alternative pathways and reduce the appeal of joining Al-Shabaab.

Education also plays a crucial role in countering radicalization. Al-Shabaab has exploited the weak education system in Somalia to indoctrinate and recruit young minds. Therefore, efforts should be made to improve access to quality education, promote critical thinking, and religious tolerance. Educational initiatives should emphasize peace-building, tolerance, and civic engagement to counter the extremist narrative.

Furthermore, addressing the grievances of marginalized communities is essential. Ethnic, clan, and regional tensions have been exploited by Al-Shabaab to gain support. Efforts should be made to foster inclusivity, promote dialogue, and address grievances through a comprehensive reconciliation process. Involving local communities, religious leaders, and civil society organizations in this process is crucial for sustainable peace.

It is also important to counter the extremist ideology propagated by Al-Shabaab. This can be done through religious leaders, scholars, and community influencers who have the credibility to challenge and debunk the distorted interpretations of Islam. Supporting moderate voices within the Somali society and promoting interfaith dialogue can help undermine the extremist narrative.

In conclusion, addressing the root causes of extremism and radicalization is vital to effectively combat Al-Shabaab in Somalia. Military interventions alone cannot solve the problem. By focusing on political stability, economic development, education, community engagement, and countering extremist ideology, a comprehensive approach can be adopted that tackles the underlying factors that contribute to the rise of Al-Shabaab. Only through such efforts can a sustainable and lasting peace be achieved in Somalia.

Chapter 4: Legal and Ethical Considerations Surrounding U.S. Military Interventions

International Legal Frameworks and Justifications for U.S. Military Actions

The Battle for Somalia: Evaluating U.S. Military Interventions in the Fight Against Al-Shabaab

Introduction:

As military historians, it is crucial to understand the international legal frameworks and justifications for U.S. military actions in Somalia, specifically in combating the extremist group Al-Shabaab. This subchapter aims to explore the legal and ethical considerations that have shaped and guided these interventions, providing a comprehensive understanding of the U.S. military's role in this complex conflict.

International Legal Frameworks:

U.S. military interventions in Somalia have been conducted within the framework of international law. The United Nations Charter, particularly Article 51, grants nations the inherent right to self-defense against armed attacks. The U.S. has invoked this principle to justify its military actions in response to Al-Shabaab's attacks and the threat it poses to regional stability.

Additionally, the Authorization for Use of Military Force (AUMF) passed by the U.S. Congress in 2001, following the 9/11 attacks, has been used to justify military interventions in Somalia. The AUMF grants the President the authority to use force against any group or individual involved in the planning, authorization, or perpetration of terrorist attacks against the United States.

Justifications for U.S. Military Interventions:

The U.S. military interventions in Somalia have been justified on multiple grounds. Firstly, the interventions aim to degrade and dismantle Al-Shabaab's capabilities to plan and execute terrorist attacks, not only within Somalia but also against U.S. interests and allies. This objective aligns with the broader U.S. counterterrorism strategy to prevent the spread of extremism and protect national security.

Furthermore, the interventions seek to support the Federal Government of Somalia, which has requested assistance in combating Al-Shabaab. The U.S. military's involvement is aimed at strengthening the capacity of Somali security forces, enhancing their ability to maintain stability and establish governance structures in the country.

Legal and Ethical Considerations:

While U.S. military interventions have been conducted within legal frameworks, concerns regarding civilian casualties and humanitarian consequences persist. Strict adherence to the principles of distinction, proportionality, and precaution is essential to minimize harm to non-combatants and infrastructure. However, the complex nature of the conflict poses challenges and increases the risk of unintended collateral damage.

Additionally, the long-term implications of U.S. military interventions should be carefully assessed. It is crucial to balance short-term gains against potential long-term consequences, such as the unintended exacerbation of grievances that fuel extremism. Evaluating the effectiveness and success of U.S. efforts in combating Al-Shabaab requires a comprehensive analysis of both military and non-military strategies, including diplomatic, economic, and humanitarian initiatives.

Conclusion:

Understanding the international legal frameworks and justifications for U.S. military actions in Somalia is essential for military historians examining the role and impact of these interventions. While legal frameworks provide a basis for military interventions, ethical considerations must be continually evaluated to minimize harm to civilians and ensure long-term stability. By critically analyzing the legal and ethical dimensions of U.S. military interventions, we can gain valuable insights into the effectiveness and success of these efforts in combating Al-Shabaab and contribute to ongoing discussions surrounding counterterrorism campaigns in the region.

United Nations Security Council Resolutions

In the battle against Al-Shabaab, the United Nations Security Council (UNSC) has played a crucial role in shaping the international response and providing legal and diplomatic support to the United States' military interventions in Somalia. This subchapter explores the significance of UNSC resolutions in guiding and justifying these interventions, with a focus on their impact, effectiveness, and long-term implications.

The UNSC resolutions have served as a crucial framework for legitimizing and authorizing U.S. military interventions in Somalia. Resolution 1844, adopted in 2008, established an arms embargo on Somalia and authorized member states to use all necessary measures to combat piracy off its coast. This resolution provided the legal basis for the United States to engage in counterterrorism operations against Al-Shabaab, as the group's activities were seen as a significant threat to regional stability and international shipping routes.

Furthermore, Resolution 2093, passed in 2013, expanded the mandate of the African Union Mission in Somalia (AMISOM) to include offensive operations against Al-Shabaab. This resolution paved the way for increased involvement of U.S. forces in supporting AMISOM's efforts, including providing training, intelligence, and logistical support. The UNSC resolutions have facilitated international coordination and cooperation, enabling the United States to work alongside regional actors in combating Al-Shabaab effectively.

However, the effectiveness of these resolutions in countering Al-Shabaab has been subject to debate. While they have provided the legal framework for military interventions, the resolutions alone have not been sufficient in eradicating the group's presence in Somalia. Al-Shabaab has proven to be resilient and adaptable, exploiting political and security vacuums to regain territory and launch attacks. This raises questions about the long-term implications of U.S. military interventions and the need for a comprehensive and sustainable approach to addressing the underlying causes of extremism in Somalia.

Moreover, the UNSC resolutions have not been without their humanitarian consequences and civilian casualties. The use of airstrikes and drone strikes, often employed by the United States in its counterterrorism efforts, has resulted in collateral damage and civilian deaths. These incidents have raised ethical and legal concerns regarding the proportionality and necessity of military interventions, underscoring the importance of respecting international humanitarian law and minimizing harm to civilians.

In comparing U.S. military interventions in Somalia with other counterterrorism campaigns in the region, the role and involvement of regional actors stand out as a significant factor. The UNSC resolutions have recognized the importance of regional cooperation and integration in addressing the threat posed by Al-Shabaab. The African

Union, through AMISOM, has played a crucial role in stabilizing Somalia and combating the group. This regional involvement has helped to build local capacity, enhance political legitimacy, and establish a more sustainable framework for long-term stability.

In conclusion, the United Nations Security Council resolutions have been instrumental in guiding and justifying U.S. military interventions in Somalia to combat Al-Shabaab. While these resolutions have provided the legal basis for intervention, their effectiveness in eradicating the group's presence and achieving long-term stability remains a subject of ongoing evaluation. The humanitarian consequences and civilian casualties of military interventions underscore the importance of ethical considerations in counterterrorism efforts. Comparisons with other counterterrorism campaigns in the region highlight the significance of regional actors and cooperation in addressing the threat posed by extremist groups. Overall, a comprehensive evaluation of the UNSC resolutions is essential in understanding the impact and implications of U.S. military interventions in the fight against Al-Shabaab.

Self-Defense and Collective Security Arguments

In the battle against Al-Shabaab, the United States has justified its military interventions in Somalia using self-defense and collective security arguments. These arguments stem from the need to protect American national security interests and contribute to global stability. This subchapter explores the validity and implications of these arguments, providing military historians with valuable insights into the rationale behind U.S. military interventions in Somalia.

Under the self-defense argument, the United States maintains that Al-Shabaab poses a direct threat to its national security. With its links to international terrorist networks like Al-Qaeda, Al-Shabaab has demonstrated its ability to launch attacks against Western targets, including the deadly assault on the Westgate Mall in Nairobi. By targeting Al-Shabaab in Somalia, the U.S. aims to eliminate a potential safe haven for terrorists, disrupt their operational capabilities, and prevent attacks on American soil.

The collective security argument expands on the self-defense rationale by emphasizing the importance of international cooperation in combating terrorism. The United States contends that by intervening in Somalia, it is fulfilling its obligations as a responsible global actor, working alongside regional partners and the African Union Mission in Somalia (AMISOM) to promote stability and security in the Horn of Africa. By addressing the root causes of extremism and supporting the Somali government, the U.S. aims to prevent the spread of terrorism beyond Somalia's borders.

Critics, however, question the effectiveness and unintended consequences of these arguments. They argue that U.S. military interventions have often resulted in civilian casualties, exacerbating the very conditions that fuel extremism. Moreover, the reliance on drone strikes and other covert tactics raises legal and ethical concerns, particularly regarding the sovereignty of other nations.

To assess the validity of the self-defense and collective security arguments, it is crucial to examine the long-term implications of U.S. military interventions in Somalia. By analyzing the impact on the political landscape, humanitarian consequences, and the role of regional actors, military historians can evaluate the effectiveness and success of U.S. efforts in combating Al-Shabaab. Additionally, comparing U.S. interventions in Somalia with other counterterrorism campaigns in the region can provide valuable insights into the unique challenges and opportunities faced by the United States in the fight against extremism.

Ultimately, understanding the self-defense and collective security arguments behind U.S. military interventions in Somalia is essential for military historians studying the history and background of these interventions. By critically evaluating these arguments, historians can contribute to a comprehensive evaluation of the U.S. military's role in combating Al-Shabaab and inform future counterterrorism strategies and tactics.

Ethical Dilemmas in Targeted Killings and Counterterrorism Operations

In the complex and ever-evolving landscape of counterterrorism operations, targeted killings have become an integral part of the United States' military interventions in Somalia to combat the extremist group Al-Shabaab. However, the utilization of such tactics has raised profound ethical dilemmas that demand careful consideration and analysis.

Targeted killings involve the deliberate elimination of specific individuals who pose a threat to national security, often carried out through drone strikes or special operations. While these operations may effectively neutralize high-value targets and disrupt Al-Shabaab's operations, they present ethical challenges that military historians must explore.

One of the primary ethical dilemmas in targeted killings is the issue of proportionality. The use of force must be proportionate to the threat posed, and collateral damage should be minimized. However, in the context of Somalia, where the enemy often operates within civilian populations, striking a balance between neutralizing threats and protecting innocent lives becomes increasingly challenging. The potential for civilian casualties raises questions about the moral and legal implications of these operations.

Another ethical dilemma arises from the question of accountability. The secrecy surrounding targeted killings and the lack of transparency in their execution make it difficult to hold decision-makers responsible for their actions. The absence of clear guidelines and oversight mechanisms further complicates the ethical framework within which these operations are conducted.

Furthermore, the long-term implications of targeted killings must be evaluated. While they may offer short-term gains in dismantling Al-Shabaab's leadership, they can also deepen resentment and fuel recruitment for extremist groups. The unintended consequences of these operations on the political landscape and stability in Somalia must be carefully examined.

Additionally, the ethical considerations surrounding targeted killings extend beyond the immediate operational context. The legitimacy of such actions under international law and their compatibility with human rights standards require thorough examination. Military historians should delve into the legal framework surrounding targeted killings to critically assess their ethical standing.

Comparative analysis with other counterterrorism campaigns in the region is crucial in understanding the unique ethical challenges posed by targeted killings in Somalia. By evaluating the approaches taken in similar contexts, military historians can gain insights into the ethical dilemmas inherent in these operations and craft a comprehensive understanding of their implications.

In conclusion, the ethical dilemmas surrounding targeted killings and counterterrorism operations in Somalia demand rigorous examination. Military historians must explore issues of proportionality, accountability, long-term consequences, legal frameworks, and comparative analysis to provide a comprehensive evaluation of the ethical considerations at play. By doing so, they contribute to a deeper understanding of the complexities of U.S. military interventions in Somalia and their impact on the fight against Al-Shabaab.

Proportionality and the Protection of Civilian Lives

In the complex landscape of military interventions, the delicate balance between achieving strategic objectives and safeguarding civilian lives is of paramount importance. This subchapter delves into the critical issue of proportionality and the protection of civilian lives within the context of U.S. military interventions in Somalia to combat the extremist group Al-Shabaab.

U.S. military historians examining the history and background of military interventions in Somalia will find this subchapter particularly insightful. It sheds light on how the concept of proportionality has evolved over time, from the early stages of U.S. involvement in Somalia to the more recent counterterrorism efforts against Al-Shabaab. By analyzing the rationales behind specific military strategies and tactics employed, historians can gain a comprehensive understanding of the decision-making process and the ethical considerations at play.

The subchapter also addresses the humanitarian consequences and civilian casualties resulting from U.S. military interventions. By meticulously examining the impact on civilian lives, military historians can evaluate the effectiveness and success of U.S. efforts in combating Al-Shabaab. This evaluation allows for a nuanced understanding of the challenges faced by the U.S. military and provides valuable lessons for future interventions.

Furthermore, the subchapter explores the legal and ethical considerations surrounding U.S. military interventions in Somalia. It delves into the rules of engagement, international humanitarian law, and the ethical dilemmas faced by military personnel on the ground. Military historians will gain insights into the complexities of balancing military objectives and the protection of civilian lives, offering a critical perspective on the long-term implications of U.S. military interventions.

By comparing U.S. military interventions in Somalia with other counterterrorism campaigns in the region, this subchapter provides a broader context for analysis. It highlights similarities and differences in strategies, tactics, and outcomes, enabling military historians to draw valuable lessons from past interventions.

Ultimately, this subchapter serves as a comprehensive examination of the concept of proportionality and the protection of civilian lives within the framework of U.S. military interventions in Somalia. By addressing the legal, ethical, and strategic aspects, it offers military historians a nuanced understanding of the challenges and implications associated with combating Al-Shabaab.

Torture, Detention, and Human Rights Concerns

The issue of torture, detention, and human rights concerns has been a significant aspect of the U.S. military interventions in Somalia to combat the extremist group Al-Shabaab. This subchapter aims to address the complex and sensitive nature of these concerns, providing a comprehensive evaluation for military historians and those interested in understanding the various facets of U.S. military interventions in Somalia.

Throughout the history and background of U.S. military interventions in Somalia, allegations of torture and unlawful detention have emerged. These allegations have raised serious human rights concerns and have been met with both support and criticism from different perspectives. By exploring the origins, ideology, and operations of Al-Shabaab in Somalia, we can gain a better understanding of the context in which these allegations have arisen.

U.S. counterterrorism strategies and tactics employed against Al-Shabaab have included intelligence gathering, targeted airstrikes, and support for local forces. While these measures have undoubtedly disrupted Al-Shabaab's activities, they have also led to unintended consequences, including civilian casualties and humanitarian crises. It is crucial to analyze the humanitarian consequences and civilian casualties resulting from U.S. military interventions to assess the overall impact on the political landscape in Somalia.

One of the key areas of examination is the effectiveness and success of U.S. efforts in combating Al-Shabaab. This analysis must take into account the role and involvement of regional actors, such as the African Union Mission in Somalia (AMISOM), and their collaboration with U.S. forces. Additionally, assessing the long-term implications of U.S. military interventions in Somalia is essential to understanding the broader consequences of these actions.

The legal and ethical considerations surrounding U.S. military interventions cannot be overlooked. International human rights law and the Geneva Conventions set clear standards for the treatment of detainees and the prohibition of torture. Evaluating whether these standards have been upheld or violated is vital in providing a comprehensive analysis of the interventions in Somalia.

Finally, comparing U.S. military interventions in Somalia with other counterterrorism campaigns in the region can provide valuable insights into the strengths and weaknesses of different approaches. By examining the similarities and differences, we can gain a more nuanced understanding of the challenges faced and the lessons learned in combating extremist groups.

In conclusion, this subchapter on torture, detention, and human rights concerns aims to provide military historians and those interested in U.S. military interventions in Somalia with a comprehensive evaluation of the complex issues surrounding these interventions. By addressing all the relevant aspects, including their historical context, ethical considerations, and long-term implications, we can gain a deeper understanding of the successes, failures, and challenges encountered in the battle against Al-Shabaab.

Chapter 5: Comparison of U.S. Military Interventions in Somalia with Other Counterterrorism Campaigns in the Region

Lessons Learned from U.S. Military Interventions in Somalia

The U.S. military interventions in Somalia to combat the extremist group Al-Shabaab have had significant implications for the region and beyond. As military historians, it is crucial to examine these interventions and draw valuable lessons from them. This subchapter aims to evaluate the effectiveness and success of U.S. efforts, analyze the impact on the political landscape, assess long-term implications, and consider legal and ethical considerations.

One of the key lessons learned is the importance of understanding the history and background of a conflict before intervening militarily. The U.S. interventions in Somalia were influenced by a complex web of tribal rivalries, political instability, and historical grievances. It became evident that a comprehensive understanding of the local dynamics is crucial for achieving desired outcomes.

Additionally, the origins, ideology, and operations of Al-Shabaab must be thoroughly understood. Al-Shabaab emerged as an offshoot of the Islamic Courts Union and capitalized on political instability to gain control over large parts of Somalia. The U.S. interventions primarily focused on direct military action against the group, but this approach did not effectively address the underlying causes that allowed Al-Shabaab to thrive.

The counterterrorism strategies and tactics employed by the U.S. played a significant role in the fight against Al-Shabaab. However, it became clear that a purely military approach was insufficient. Efforts should have been made to engage with local communities, address grievances, and support institutions capable of providing security and governance.

The impact of U.S. interventions on the political landscape in Somalia was mixed. While some progress was made in weakening Al-Shabaab, it also led to unintended consequences such as increased radicalization and recruitment. The long-term implications of these interventions must be carefully assessed to avoid exacerbating the conflict further.

The humanitarian consequences and civilian casualties of U.S. military interventions cannot be ignored. It is imperative to prioritize the protection of civilians and ensure that military operations minimize collateral damage. Lessons from Somalia can inform the development of more ethical and effective military strategies in future interventions.

Furthermore, the role and involvement of regional actors in U.S. military interventions should be carefully considered. Collaboration and coordination with regional partners are crucial for achieving sustainable stability in Somalia. Examining the successes and challenges of such partnerships can provide valuable insights.

Finally, it is essential to compare U.S. military interventions in Somalia with other counterterrorism campaigns in the region. By analyzing similarities and differences, military historians can draw broader conclusions and identify best practices for future interventions.

In conclusion, the U.S. military interventions in Somalia have yielded important lessons for military historians and those interested in understanding the complexities of counterterrorism efforts. By critically evaluating the effectiveness and success of these interventions, analyzing the impact on the political landscape, and considering legal and ethical considerations, valuable insights can be gained for future military interventions.

Successes and Failures in Achieving Objectives

In the ongoing battle against Al-Shabaab in Somalia, the United States has experienced both successes and failures in achieving its objectives. This subchapter aims to critically evaluate these outcomes and shed light on the effectiveness of U.S. military interventions in combating this extremist group.

One of the key successes of U.S. military interventions in Somalia has been the disruption of Al-Shabaab's operational capacity. Through targeted airstrikes and special operations, the U.S. has successfully eliminated key leaders and disrupted their command structure. This has significantly hindered Al-Shabaab's ability to carry out large-scale attacks and maintain control over territory. Additionally, the U.S. has provided training and support to the Somali National Army, enabling them to take the lead in counterinsurgency operations against the group.

However, there have also been notable failures in achieving objectives. Despite years of military intervention, Al-Shabaab remains a resilient and potent force in Somalia. The group continues to carry out deadly attacks, both within Somalia and in neighboring countries. This raises questions about the effectiveness of U.S. counterterrorism strategies and tactics employed against Al-Shabaab. It is crucial to analyze and learn from these failures to ensure a more successful approach in the future.

The impact of U.S. military interventions on the political landscape in Somalia is another important aspect to consider. While the interventions have aimed to stabilize the country and foster a functioning government, the results have been mixed. The Somali government has struggled to establish control and unity, and political instability persists. Furthermore, there have been concerns about the humanitarian consequences and civilian casualties resulting from U.S.

military interventions. This raises ethical considerations and questions about the long-term implications of these interventions.

It is also crucial to assess the role and involvement of regional actors in U.S. military interventions. The support and cooperation of neighboring countries such as Kenya and Ethiopia have been instrumental in the fight against Al-Shabaab. However, there have been instances where regional actors have pursued their own interests, which may have undermined the overall objectives of the U.S. interventions.

To gain a comprehensive understanding, it is important to compare U.S. military interventions in Somalia with other counterterrorism campaigns in the region. This analysis allows for a broader perspective on the successes and failures of U.S. efforts, drawing valuable lessons from similar campaigns.

In conclusion, the successes and failures in achieving objectives in U.S. military interventions against Al-Shabaab in Somalia have had significant implications for the country's political landscape, humanitarian situation, and regional dynamics. By critically evaluating these outcomes, military historians can contribute to a deeper understanding of the effectiveness and long-term implications of U.S. interventions, fostering informed discussions and potentially shaping future strategies in combating extremist groups.

Adaptation of Strategies and Tactics

The adaptation of strategies and tactics has played a crucial role in the U.S. military interventions in Somalia to combat the extremist group Al-Shabaab. This subchapter aims to delve into the various ways in which the U.S. military has adjusted its approach over time to effectively address the evolving challenges posed by Al-Shabaab.

From the early stages of U.S. military interventions in Somalia to the present day, the strategies and tactics employed have undergone significant modifications. Initially, the focus was primarily on direct military intervention and support to the Somali government forces in targeting Al-Shabaab strongholds. However, it soon became evident that a purely kinetic approach was insufficient in dismantling the group. As a result, the U.S. military shifted its strategy towards a more comprehensive and holistic approach, encompassing not only military operations but also counterinsurgency efforts, intelligence gathering, and capacity building of Somali security forces.

One key adaptation has been the utilization of targeted airstrikes against high-value Al-Shabaab leaders and infrastructure. These precision strikes have been instrumental in disrupting the group's command structure and impeding their operational capabilities. Coupled with enhanced intelligence sharing and coordination with regional actors, such as the African Union Mission in Somalia (AMISOM), these tactics have yielded significant successes in degrading Al-Shabaab's operational capacity.

Furthermore, the U.S. military has recognized the importance of integrating traditional military operations with non-kinetic approaches. This includes engaging in civil-military cooperation, supporting local governance and development initiatives, and providing humanitarian assistance to win over the hearts and minds of the Somali population. By addressing the root causes of extremism and offering tangible alternatives, the U.S. military seeks to undermine Al-Shabaab's appeal and recruitment efforts.

The adaptability of U.S. strategies and tactics has also extended to the use of unmanned aerial vehicles (UAVs) or drones. These technological advancements have revolutionized intelligence gathering and surveillance capabilities, enabling the U.S. military to gather real-time information, identify high-value targets, and minimize the risks to its personnel.

However, it is worth noting that the adaptation of strategies and tactics has not been without its challenges. The complex and fluid nature of the Somali conflict, coupled with the presence of other armed groups and the interplay of regional dynamics, has necessitated constant reassessment and adjustment of approaches. Moreover, there is a need to balance the short-term military gains with the long-term political and humanitarian implications of military interventions.

In conclusion, the U.S. military interventions in Somalia have witnessed a significant adaptation of strategies and tactics over time. From a purely kinetic approach to a comprehensive counterinsurgency strategy, the U.S. military has demonstrated flexibility and adaptability in its fight against Al-Shabaab. By incorporating targeted airstrikes, intelligence sharing, civil-military cooperation, and technological advancements, the U.S. military has made significant progress in combating the extremist group. However, the challenges posed by the evolving nature of the conflict and the wider political landscape in Somalia necessitate constant reassessment and adjustment of strategies and tactics to achieve long-term stability and security in the region.

Comparative Analysis of U.S. Efforts in Somalia, Yemen, and Afghanistan

In this subchapter, we will conduct a comparative analysis of U.S. efforts in Somalia, Yemen, and Afghanistan in order to provide military historians with a comprehensive understanding of the challenges and successes faced by the United States in its counterterrorism campaigns. By examining these three distinct cases, we can identify commonalities, differences, and lessons learned that can inform future military interventions.

Starting with Somalia, the U.S. military interventions in this country have been primarily aimed at combating the extremist group Al-Shabaab. We will delve into the history and background of these interventions, exploring the motivations and objectives that led to U.S. involvement. Understanding Al-Shabaab's origins, ideology, and operations within Somalia is crucial to comprehending the complex dynamics at play.

Next, we will evaluate the various counterterrorism strategies and tactics employed by the U.S. against Al-Shabaab. This will involve analyzing the effectiveness and success of these efforts, considering factors such as drone strikes, training and equipping local forces, and intelligence sharing. We will also assess the impact of these interventions on the political landscape in Somalia, including their influence on governance and stability.

Examining the humanitarian consequences and civilian casualties resulting from U.S. military interventions is of utmost importance. We will critically analyze the ethical implications of these actions, exploring the legal and moral considerations that should underpin such interventions. By doing so, we can evaluate the extent to which the U.S. has prioritized the protection of civilian lives in its fight against Al-Shabaab.

To provide a broader perspective, we will compare the U.S. military interventions in Somalia with its counterterrorism campaigns in Yemen and Afghanistan. By examining similarities and differences in objectives, strategies, and outcomes, we can identify key lessons and best practices that can inform future military interventions in the region.

Finally, we will assess the long-term implications of U.S. military interventions in Somalia, considering both intended and unintended consequences. This will involve analyzing the role and involvement of regional actors in these intershtions, as well as the potential for sustainable peace and stability in the region.

Overall, this subchapter aims to provide military historians with a comprehensive and nuanced understanding of U.S. efforts in Somalia, Yemen, and Afghanistan. By examining these cases from multiple angles, we can gain valuable insights into the challenges and successes of counterterrorism campaigns and inform future military interventions in the fight against extremist groups.

Similarities and Differences in Extremist Threats

Understanding the similarities and differences in extremist threats is crucial in evaluating U.S. military interventions in the fight against Al-Shabaab in Somalia. This subchapter explores the various aspects of extremist threats and draws comparisons with other counterterrorism campaigns in the region.

One key similarity among extremist threats is their ideological foundation. Al-Shabaab, much like other extremist groups, is driven by a radical interpretation of Islam that seeks to establish a strict Islamic state. This common ideology creates a shared enemy for the United States and its regional partners, making it easier to coordinate efforts against these groups.

However, differences arise when examining the origins and operations of these extremist organizations. Al-Shabaab, for instance, emerged from the ashes of the Islamic Courts Union (ICU) in Somalia, which was initially formed to restore law and order. Over time, the ICU's radical elements gained prominence, leading to the birth of Al-Shabaab. This unique trajectory sets Al-Shabaab apart from other extremist groups, such as Boko Haram or Al-Qaeda in the Arabian Peninsula, which evolved under different circumstances.

Furthermore, Al-Shabaab's operations in Somalia are distinct in their focus on local governance and territorial control. Unlike some other extremist groups that primarily engage in high-profile attacks,

Al-Shabaab seeks to establish itself as a governing authority and enforce a strict interpretation of Sharia law. This governance aspect poses its own set of challenges for U.S. military interventions, as it requires a multifaceted approach that goes beyond conventional counterterrorism tactics.

Comparing U.S. military interventions in Somalia with other counterterrorism campaigns in the region sheds light on the effectiveness and success of these efforts. The challenges faced by the U.S. in Somalia, such as a weak central government and a complex clan-based society, are not unique to the region. Similar dynamics have been observed in Yemen, Iraq, and Afghanistan, where U.S. interventions have also encountered obstacles in achieving lasting stability.

Understanding the similarities and differences in extremist threats is crucial for military historians evaluating U.S. military interventions in the fight against Al-Shabaab. By examining the ideological foundations, origins, operations, and approaches used in countering these threats, a comprehensive assessment can be made regarding the effectiveness and long-term implications of these interventions. Furthermore, comparing these interventions with other counterterrorism campaigns in the region provides valuable insights into the broader challenges faced by the U.S. and its regional partners in combating extremism.

5. Impact of U.S. Military Interventions on the Political Landscape in Somalia

The political landscape in Somalia has been significantly shaped by U.S. military interventions in its fight against the extremist group Al-Shabaab. This subchapter aims to evaluate the impact of these interventions on the political dynamics within the country.

Since the early 1990s, Somalia has experienced political instability and a lack of effective governance. The presence of Al-Shabaab further exacerbated this situation, posing a threat to regional stability and U.S. national security interests. In response, the United States initiated military interventions with the objective of combating Al-Shabaab and promoting stability in Somalia.

One of the key impacts of U.S. military interventions has been the support provided to the Federal Government of Somalia (FGS) and the African Union Mission in Somalia (AMISOM). Through training, equipment provision, and advisory support, the United States has played a crucial role in strengthening the capabilities of the FGS and AMISOM forces. This has resulted in increased territorial gains against Al-Shabaab and improved security in certain areas.

However, challenges remain in achieving sustainable political stability. The political landscape in Somalia remains fragmented, with various clans, regional authorities, and armed groups vying for power and resources. The U.S. interventions, while successful in weakening Al-Shabaab, have not fully addressed the underlying political grievances and divisions within the country.

Furthermore, concerns have been raised about the potential for U.S. interventions to inadvertently exacerbate existing tensions. The United States has primarily supported the central government, which has led to accusations of favoritism and marginalization from other actors. This has the potential to further polarize the political landscape and hinder efforts towards reconciliation and inclusive governance.

Another important aspect to consider is the role of regional actors in U.S. military interventions. Countries such as Kenya and Ethiopia have been involved in cross-border operations against Al-Shabaab, often with the support of the United States. While this regional cooperation has been instrumental in countering the extremist group, it has also contributed to regional rivalries and tensions that have spilled over into Somalia.

In conclusion, U.S. military interventions in Somalia have had a significant impact on the country's political landscape. While there have been successes in weakening Al-Shabaab and supporting the FGS and AMISOM, challenges persist in achieving lasting political stability. The involvement of regional actors and the need for inclusive governance remain critical factors to consider. It is essential for military historians to evaluate the long-term implications of these interventions on the political dynamics in Somalia and to draw lessons from the successes and failures of U.S. efforts in combating Al-Shabaab. Additionally, a comparison with other counterterrorism campaigns in the region can provide valuable insights into effective strategies and tactics for future interventions.